YOUR MARRIAGE MATTERS

By Jeremy & Corrie Isaacs

Editor: Karen Snyder
Cover Design: Garret Snyder

Thanks for picking up this book. We view writing as an extension of the ministry God has given to us, first in our home, second in our local church, Generations Church, and third through speaking at conferences and events.

If we can serve your church or ministry at an event or by offering bulk discounts on the book for small groups and other ministry efforts please don't hesitate to reach out to us by email: **jeremycorrieisaacs@gmail.com**

Other books from Jeremy:

You're Not as Good as They Say You Are, but You're Not That Bad Either (2009)

Toxic Soul: A Pastor's Guide to Leading without Losing Heart (2017)

ENDORSEMENTS

If you want a first hand view of real with a dash of fun and laughter, Jeremy and Corrie do just that. They have the ability to draw people to them for their authenticity and genuine care and concern for where you are in your journey of life! Jeremy is a husband and father like no other (in our opinion) and Corrie is a wife and mother that sets her love and passion for her family. We love to hear their stories...not just because we laugh until the body hurts...but due to the knowledge shared, resolve, solutions, and wisdom concerning everyday life and marriage.

Bill & Shelley Isaacs
Lake Erie Church (Madison, OH)

After nearly 20 years of marriage Jeremy and Corrie still actually like each other. We would know; we've been there the entire time. We've watched them date, marry, have kids, and raise teenagers, and in every season they have modeled integrity, patience, and a genuine love for each other. Those are the kind of marriage books we want to read: books written by people who do what they say and say what they do. That is Jeremy and Corrie all the way.

Jason & Andrea Isaacs
Hope City Church (Louisville, KY)

Jeremy and Corrie Isaacs have written a practical guide on how to successfully navigate the most satisfying and frustrating relationship on earth. They masterfully interweave scripture with their own personal experiences and wise insights to provide an entertaining yet realistic look at marriage. The Isaacs paint a transparent and honest portrait of the marital union that is refreshing and inspiring. Knowing Jeremy and Corrie personally, we have had the privilege of seeing their marriage up close and it is the real deal. Any married or engaged couple owe it to themselves to read this book – because "Your Marriage Matters."

Mark and Udella Walker
Lee University (Cleveland, TN)

*God placed an emphasis on the importance of marriage and family (Genesis 2:18, 2:24). That is one of the reasons satan is constantly after your marriage. The enemy hates what God loves! "Your Marriage Matters" is an exceptional and necessary resource to help strengthen, encourage, and equip you to fight for your marriage – no matter the season. Jeremy and Corrie not only provide practical ways for us to invest into our marriage, but their transparent and genuine stories will keep you reeled in from start to finish! As you read this book you **WILL** laugh and you **MAY** cry as you are constantly reminded you are married ON purpose and FOR a purpose and that, "Your Marriage Matters!" EVERY MARRIED COUPLE NEEDS THIS BOOK!*

JC & Kimberly Worley
GO Church (Georgia & Maryland)

If your marriage needs a spark, every day practices, a good laugh & more of Jesus, then "Your Marriage Matters" is a must read. The best part of this book is that each chapter is not just a good idea but something that Jeremy & Corrie live out daily together. My wife and I have watched, learned & implemented many of the concepts written about in this fun and easy to read book & our marriage is better today because of them.

Kyle & Jennifer Jackson
Church of the Highlands (Columbus, GA)

Great marriages are not fallen into, they are fought for! In this book, Jeremy & Corrie give a beautiful roadmap of what it looks like to fight for a marriage worth having. More than that - they show you that your marriage can in fact get better and better over the years. Their words will inspire you, make you laugh and challenge you to keep believing that your marriage matters. If your desire is to be a part of a God-centered, committed & intentional marriage...this book will undoubtedly help you.

Noah & Maddy Herrin
Way Church (Nashville, TN)

During the Tennessee blizzard of 1993, Christal and I were joined together in wedded bliss. Four children, four grandchildren, twelve houses, seven states, and millions of memories later, we've reached an absolutely fantastic stage. Not only can we attest to the monumental truths found in "Your Marriage Matters," but within it, we've also found a wonderful resource to point others to as well.

We've had the privilege of knowing the Isaacs for many years and have always been impressed by their balance of wisdom and wit. In fact, balance would be a good descriptive word of what they model to those around them in their lives, marriage, and ministry.

Using honesty and transparency combined with practical tips, personal snapshots from their lives, and a firm biblical foundation, Jeremy and Corrie have penned a masterstroke for your marriage. We recommend that you sit down with your spouse, take your time and dig deep within the pages of this book. Allow it to be not only a resource but also a reminder of how important your marriage truly is. We're cheering you on!

Rob & Christal Bailey
Church of God Youth & Discipleship (Cleveland, TN)

We've watched as Jeremy and Corrie have lived out the message of this book through life's battles and ups and downs. They have moral authority to share this message. Be careful. This book could change your life...and your marriage!

Shawn & Tricia Lovejoy
Courage to Lead (Birmingham, AL)

Not only are Jeremy and Corrie Isaacs some of our favorite people in the world, they have become one of our go-to couples when speaking into marriages. Now, with this amazing book, you will understand why. They are insightful, funny, real, and wise beyond their years. They don't pretend to have it all together, but what they do have is a deep well of insight and experience that will make a huge difference in your marriage too.

Arvil & Cheryl Ogle
Intentional Family (Alpharetta, GA)

DEDICATION

This book is dedicated to our parents. They pointed us to Jesus, they have loved us unconditionally, and they offer to watch the grandkids from time to time so we can invest in our own marriage.

FOREWORD

Everyone has blind spots. One beautiful aspect of God's perfect design for marriage is that both spouses can help each other avoid blind spots and pitfalls. I (Dave) had a blind spot recently which Ashley lovingly helped me to correct. We were walking through the aisles of Target doing some shopping when Ashley put her arm around me and placed something into the cart while she lovingly whispered in my ear, "Trust me. It's time for this."

I looked down into the cart and saw that the item she had placed there was an electric nose hair trimmer. I laughed at first thinking it was a joke, but then I discreetly reached up to my upper lip to discover that indeed I had the beginnings of a mustache emerging from my nostrils. She helped me see a blind spot.

Some blind spots are as innocuous as a few unsightly nose hairs, while other blind spots can be less visible but more dangerous. When our habits, our mindsets or our choices start to veer off course into an unhealthy direction, a wise spouse will help you see the situation from a new perspective. A loving spouse will tell you the truth; and even when it may be a difficult truth to hear, it will be given with both honesty and tenderness. Tenderhearted transparency is an often overlooked secret to lifelong love.

Some couples master the art of "honesty," but they have no tenderness. They act as if criticism was a spiritual gift. For the record, criticism is not a spiritual gift, but encouragement is still on the list. A critical spouse will use their so-called honesty as a weapon to wound their spouse instead of a gift to encourage their spouse. They hurl corrective insults from a posture of power as if it was their job to correct, shape and referee every aspect of their spouse's life. They are fluent in the languages of nagging, criticism, and sarcasm.

Other couples are great at the tenderness part, but they forget the transparency. They're afraid of awkward conversations, so they hold back on the honesty. They pretend issues don't really exist. They seem incapable of sharing the whole truth. They always seem to be saying everything is "fine," but for them, "F.I.N.E" really means they're Faking, Ignoring, Neglecting and Evading the truth and the real issues.

I (Ashley) used to overuse the word "fine" to avoid talking about how I was really feeling. I believed the myth that Dave should be able to read my mind and perfectly interpret my nonverbal cues to know that I wasn't really fine. When he failed to pick up on my telepathic messages, I'd get frustrated with him and then he'd be confused by my bad mood. This exhausting cycle continued until I finally found the courage to share what was really on my heart, and it changed everything for the better.

Maybe, like us, you've struggled with communication in marriage, but you don't have to stay stuck in a negative cycle. Perhaps, like us, you've been living with blind spots that are causing harm to your marriage. Thankfully, you also don't have to figure out the solutions on your own. The Bible gives us a proven recipe for healthy communication.

In the book you're about to read, our friends Jeremy and Corrie Isaacs have created a beautiful roadmap to help you navigate the journey of marriage. Through their raw honesty about their own struggles, their hilarious wit, their pastoral hearts, and their Biblical instruction, they will bring you encouragement and practical tips for whatever season of marriage you might currently be facing. We are so thankful for their ministry, their authenticity, and this powerful book they've written together.

We believe you have not picked up this book by accident. We believe God has led you to this moment and this book you're now holding is an important tool to help you grow as a couple. If you'll read this book while also praying for God to reveal your own blind spots and to give you wisdom to know how to apply the lessons you're learning, we believe those prayers combined with the wisdom on the pages to come will have a life-changing impact for you and your spouse. We are praying for you and cheering you on as you begin this journey!

Thank you to our friends, the Isaacs, for creating this inspiring resource and inviting us to be part of it by writing this foreword. Thank you, Reader, for taking time to invest in your marriage by reading it. God has big plans for you! The best is yet to come.

Dave and Ashley Willis
Pastors, Authors, and Hosts of *The Naked Marriage Podcast*

Table of Contents

ONCE UPON A TIME

I (Jeremy) come from an incredible picture of marriage health. My parents were married for nearly 33 years prior to my mom's passing at just 48 years old. Now if you can do the math, they got married really young. In fact, mom and dad were dating and got engaged while she was 15. As the story goes, dad was trying to work up the nerve to ask my mom's dad for his daughter's "hand in marriage." The two men were up late playing cards one night when dad finally popped the question: "Paul, would it be okay with you if I asked Kathy to marry me?"

My grandfather pushed back from the table, totally prepared for the question and having already processed his answer.

"Bill, you have my permission on two conditions. First, you have to let her call home whenever she wants. Second, you have to let her have all the Coca-Cola she ever wants. Can you do those two things?"

My dad got his heart to slow down just enough to answer yes, he could do those two things. They waited until mom turned 16 and about two months after her birthday they got married.

I'm not sure great marriages are built on those two principles, but maybe my grandfather knew something others didn't know, because it worked. I was born a few years after that conversation, my brother a few years after that, and while it wasn't the perfect marriage, it was a really great one to grow up around.

I never heard my parents fight. I found out later their code words were "Can we go talk about the budget?" That was the indication that one or the other of them needed to go behind closed doors to express some varying level of frustration. I just thought they were really diligent with our family finances. Regardless, the home was filled with peace. Each of my parents were affectionate toward the other publicly, but not uncomfortably so. They also both spoke highly of the other inside and outside the home.

I don't ever remember mom or dad sitting me or my brother, Jason, down and saying, "Here's how to have a healthy marriage." We just watched and listened and learned.

My grandparents on both sides were married until death parted them. My aunts and uncles, cousins, even distant relatives seemed to have healthy and happy marriages for the most part. I never really considered divorce in any of the relationships close to me until I was much older than my friends who had endured a different picture of marriage their whole lives.

When Corrie and I were planning our wedding and the joining of our lives together, I felt very prepared for marriage.

— — — — —

My (Corrie) context of marriage was almost the polar opposite. My mom is an amazing woman who loves the Lord and kept us in church our whole lives (more on this later). However, she would be the first to tell you that her luck in love wasn't all that good.

She was married a few times preceding my arrival to the world, and two more over the remainder of my "growing up years." When you take each relationship separately, they all make sense, and unfortunately, she was the innocent party at nearly every turn. And yet, I didn't have the steady marital influence in my childhood that Jeremy did.

For the most part, I was raised in the house of a single mom, with two sisters. Four girls living under one roof. Most of our friends just called us "The Monroe Girls." It wasn't uncommon for us to show up to the house and some of our friends were already there, having let themselves in. It was the place to be.

If you walked in on any given day, you might assume that some combination of us were fighting. We were usually just communicating passionately. Did I mention that most of my life all four of us lived in a two-bedroom, one-bathroom duplex? Four girls. One bathroom. Looking back, I'm not entirely sure I know how we all got ready for school or church or a dance. But we did.

Mom was in one long-term dating relationship during my childhood and early teen years. Ironically, she didn't marry him, but it was a serious relationship. We still talk fondly about that guy, but mom knew she wasn't supposed to marry him. So even though he asked several times, she just couldn't do it. He had the means to improve our lives financially. He even asked to do so when they were breaking up for the last time, but mom said no. I respect her so much for her conviction in that relationship.

When I think back on the marriages of my relatives and close family friends, it was a mixed bag. There were a few I was able to watch up close who showed me what it looked like to be in committed, loving relationships. Others fell in and out of love throughout my life. Still others *were* married, but the relationship didn't seem fulfilling or healthy for one or both parties.

Needless to say, I couldn't really walk into my marriage to Jeremy with a lot of confidence that what I had experienced at home would set me up for success. I did feel confident, but that confidence came from somewhere else.

— — — —

As of the writing of this book, we have been married almost 19 years and have four kids. We do not have a perfect marriage. We have a great marriage, but we argue and fight about the same things most couples we know argue about. We get stressed and take it out on the other far too often. No matter how hard we try, we frustrate each other and miss the mark in prioritizing the right things. We keep working because we value the gift God has given us.

We are fellow sojourners with you. Having had the chance to interact with thousands of married couples in the ministry of our local church and speaking at marriage events, we believe there are some foundational principles that will help every married couple find fulfillment and better live out the story God desires to write through their relationship.

The number one thing we want you to know is this:

Your Marriage Matters!

It matters for the reasons you probably think it matters, and it matters for more reasons than you can even imagine.

Maybe you grabbed this book because you just love the subject of marriage. You can't get enough. You guys go to every marriage conference, read every book, and listen to all the top marriage podcasts.

Maybe you grabbed this book because you're at the end of your rope. You can't be 100 percent positive they'll be there when you get home. You may not even be sure you want them to be there.

Maybe you're planning to read this by yourself, or maybe you'll read it together.

No matter your rationale or your plan, know this: We've prayed for you! Our hope and prayer is the words that fill these pages aren't just words, but they are life to you. You can do it. God has a plan for your future. You're going to make it. Our hope is it includes both you and your spouse growing closer to God and closer to each other. However, even if you feel like you're the only one fighting for the future of your marriage, keep fighting. It's worth it!

Jeremy & Corrie Isaacs
Canton, GA

FAIRYTALES AREN'T FAKE

We love to watch Hallmark-type movies and rom-coms. In fact, one of our first dates was when we were 16 or 17 and Jeremy drove from Chattanooga to Knoxville for us to see a movie. We have recorded hundreds of movies over the years to watch together once the kids go to bed or on rainy days. There have been so many times when Jeremy has fallen asleep before the movie ends (this is not a rare occurrence) and I (Corrie) will walk in the next day to find him watching the movie all by himself. He says he just wanted to catch up to where I was, but I think it's obvious he loves them as much or more than I do. We really do love them!

One of the things we love the most are the great storylines. They quit their jobs to chase after the love of their life. They fly through the night to get to one another. They stand out in the cold just waiting for a chance to say, "I love you." These are powerful expressions of love depicted on the screen.

Do you know what makes those stories unrealistic? Those characters aren't the ones choosing to do those things. There are writers who create moments and dictate behavior so the characters always do the right thing. They write it so the characters always know exactly what to say.

"You complete me" weren't words thought up in a real living room in the chaos of emotion by

Renee Zellweger in the movie *Jerry McGuire*. They were brainstormed in a room of writers, edited, honed, rehearsed, and delivered in front of lights and cameras over the course of multiple takes.

Think about your favorite line of dialogue from a movie or television show. Those characters on a screen didn't have to process all they were feeling—fear, doubt, joy, sadness, insecurity, confidence—while trying to form the perfect words to express affection to the other person.

They had writers.

You and I don't have that benefit. We have to star in our lives and write our own lines on the spot. So, in our relationships we don't always do or say the perfect thing.

But what if that wasn't true?

What if there actually was a writer for your life story and for your marriage?

We believe there is. There is someone who can help us know what to do and what to say in our relationships. We want to give you some guiding principles that might not turn your marriage into a Hallmark movie, but will definitely improve the quality of your relationship.

The closer we each get to God, the closer we get to each other.

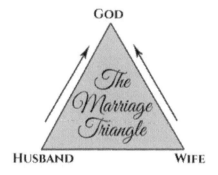

Perhaps you've seen a similar diagram to the one above. As the husband and wife move toward God, they are actually moving toward one another. The best way to experience relational closeness is to be in relationship with someone who is pursuing relational closeness with God, while you do the same.

Matthew 22:37 Jesus replied, '"You must love the Lord your God with all your heart, all your soul, and all your mind.'"

Maybe you assumed a pastor and his wife would start a marriage book by going all Jesus and the Bible on you, but we believe this is so important.

You cannot be the absolute best husband or wife to your spouse if you aren't in a growing relationship with Jesus.

There are a lot of reasons we believe this, but perhaps the most important place to start is to remember that you aren't *just* a physical person.

You are body, soul, and mind. So is your spouse. As you give God the very best of yourself, you are becoming the best version of who you are supposed to be. Therefore, you are giving the best version of you to your spouse. The inverse is true as well. As they are in pursuit of that growing relationship with Jesus too, they are giving you the best version of themselves. Without these efforts by both parties, we bring incomplete, unhealthy, unfulfilled versions of ourselves to someone else and ask them to fix us, complete us, or heal us.

Newsflash: No one else can do for you what God can do for you.

So, I give myself in growing measure to Him and as He continues to mold, shape, and make me more and more into His image, I bring a more complete and healthier version of me to my spouse.

Closing Thoughts

I (Jeremy) wasn't telling the whole truth. I wasn't really lying to Corrie, but I definitely wasn't being honest with her. I wouldn't say any of the things were big things, but in my attempt to protect her, or buy myself more time to get a better answer to something, I would give her incomplete answers or just not communicate with her altogether. We were talking, but we weren't really communicating.

One night, Corrie said, "What is going on? You seem distant. I feel like I've lost you. Where are you?"

Something in me broke. I started crying. Like the ugly cry. Like Oprah gives the family a new house and a new car and beds for all the kids kind of tears. After I got it together, I admitted to her that I hadn't been caring for my soul too well. Again, I don't want to make it sound like something it wasn't. This wasn't sin or unfaithfulness to

Corrie. This was unhealth in Jeremy. I hadn't dealt with past pain. I wasn't willing to admit some fears I was wrestling with. I couldn't bring myself to confront some insecurities that had recently arisen in me.

I didn't want to let her down, and I didn't know how to fix what was broken, so I just suppressed it all and tried to keep moving. I thought I had her fooled because I was fooling myself. Surely, she was buying it too.

She wasn't.

Those tears were the start of some healing for me. Over the course of several hours, I confessed my hurts, pain, fears, worry, shortcomings, and dishonesty. I repented to God and to Corrie. I asked for help. I created some very specific next steps and asked her to hold me accountable.

No one creates *that* Hallmark movie. These aren't kisses under the moonlight. These are tears on the bathroom floor.

This isn't the love story on TV.

This is our love story.

Who told us our story wasn't good enough? Who convinced us that we had to pretend we had it all together?

Don't buy into that lie. Be 100 percent honest with yourself. Give 100 percent of your life to Jesus. Then take your 100 percent and your spouse's 100 percent and spend a lifetime figuring out the Biblical math that says

$$1+1=1 \text{ (our paraphrase)}$$

There is a writer to your love story and His name is Jesus. Quit trying to write your own story, give Him the pen, and live the story He is writing for you. We promise, it's so much better!

COMMUNICATION

We've known each other since we were 13 years old and were best friends even prior to dating, getting engaged, and getting married. So, you would think we mastered communication prior to getting married, or surely soon thereafter. HA!

While we are so thankful for the foundation our friendship provided to our marriage, communication is an issue for every couple we've ever met, including us.

Years ago, Dr. John Gray introduced the world to the idea that *Men Are from Mars, Women Are from Venus.* The metaphor is to illustrate that we speak different languages. One of my (Jeremy) favorite movie lines of all time is from *Rush Hour* when Chris Tucker says, "Do you understand the words that are coming out of my mouth?" In context it was hilarious!

How many times in marriage is this the relevant question?

One day I came home after being gone all day to work. Corrie had been home with our young kids. Upon my arrival she said we needed a few groceries and asked if she could run to the store. I don't say that because I'm a dictatorial husband who requires her to do so, but as an Enneagram 9 she often asks instead of stating. Of course, I said yes, and she left. I'm sure I did an exceptional job "dad-ing" while she was gone. She came home, we had dinner, got the kids to bed, and later that evening we were talking. Corrie was sharing about her level of stress and frustration during that specific day. At some point in the conversation, she said, "I love the kids. I want to stay home with them. I wouldn't trade it for anything in the world, but I never get a break. Just a few minutes of 'me time'." I responded, "You just went to the grocery store."

I can literally feel every woman reading this right now trying to reach through the book and strangle me.

I get it!

Not my finest moment.

In fairness, I wasn't saying that grocery shopping or even being gone from the house for those few minutes was the "me time" she was seeking or needing. I was taking very literal her statements "I need a break" and "The kids are always with me." I know...it doesn't make sense. Even now, all these years later, that comment still has a way of coming back up in specific conversations.

I was listening, but not well. I knew what she was saying, but I didn't hear what she was saying.

Communication is just hard.

It doesn't actually matter what words the other person says, we often hear something different.

It has been said that in any conversation between two people there are at least six people present. They are:

Who I think I am
Who I think you think I am
Who I really am
Who I think you are
Who I think you think you are
Who you really are

All of our conversations are filtered through these personas. So, before the words leave my mouth, they pass through these filters in my brain as I try to communicate effectively. Then the other person's ears hear the words, and they filter it through these personas as well, and now it's like the old lunchroom game of telephone. What was said in the beginning isn't even remotely what is received.

Additionally, we aren't usually talking about insignificant things in marriage. We are talking about:

- Our kids in general
- Getting on the same page with parenting a specific situation
- How to manage our money
- Making a big financial decision
- Sex
- Fears and insecurities
- Our careers and dreams
- Brokenness and hurt

And so many other things. And there's one more BIG problem with our communication: Most of what we say aren't the words coming out of our mouth.

In *Nonverbal Communication* by Albert Mehrabian, we learn that 55 percent of our communication is body language. Before we open our mouth, the other person is reading how tense we are, what our face is communicating, are our arms crossed, are we crying, do we seem happy, etc.

Another 38 percent of our communication is the tone of our voice. So once our body communicates something, our inflection adds to their receptiveness. Are we yelling? Did our voice just break with emotion? Are we talking loudly in a public place about something personal or sensitive?

You put those two things together and 93 percent of what we are often communicating takes place without words. We struggle with words, but they are only seven percent of our communication.

Even if you are saying the most beautiful things about someone, if you do so with body language and a tone communicating something different, they won't know how to receive it. Our brains work overtime to try to interpret what is being communicated, often while bypassing our ears. Our eyes do most of the work. This is one reason it's so important to put the phones down or turn away from the TV and toward each other when you are talking to one another. Your eyes will tell you what your ears are struggling to comprehend.

Sometimes we're just talking too much. In the New Testament, the book of James encourages us to take a different approach.

James 1:19 Understand this, my dear brothers and sisters: You must all be quick to listen, slow to speak, and slow to get angry.

Could it be that our communication would drastically improve if we would just listen more and speak less?

The more words we say, the more we might have to regret. I can think of very few times in my life where I regretted being silent, but I can think of a lot of times where I regretted saying something. However, it's not just about being quiet, it's also about listening. That presents a whole new set of problems because most of us aren't very good listeners to begin with.

Be honest. How much of your listening isn't as much listening as it is preparing what to say next? Your spouse is talking about what he or she feels or thinks and, instead of actively listening to understand what they are saying, you are formulating your response. That's why we cut each other off. That's how we can start talking as soon as they take a breath. We contend—and it's been true in our marriage—the more we listen to one another, the better our marriage. The more the other person feels heard, the less defensive we each get.

Our level of anger is proportionate to the ratio of our listening and speaking. When I listen more than I speak, the less I get angry.

Visually that might look like this:

LISTENING > SPEAKING > ANGER

We aren't saying you should never speak. Obviously, there are things that need to be said. Each partner should be able to communicate what they feel without feeling like they are doing something wrong, but there is a way to say what needs to be said.

Proverbs 16:24 Gracious words are like a honeycomb, sweetness to the soul and health to the body.

*Proverbs 18:21 Death and life are in
the power of the tongue.*

Isn't it amazing that the wisest man on earth,
Solomon, who wrote the book of Proverbs, talked
so much about our words? You and I hold
enormous power with our words. We often say,
"You can say the right thing but say it the wrong
way." You can be right and still be wrong.

When you speak, speak *life.* Let your words
speak life into your spouse. Let them speak life
to your children, to your grandchildren, and to
your coworkers.

People won't remember what you said, but they'll
remember how you made them feel. Breath life.
Speak life. Speak encouragement. Your partner
should never have to go to someone else to hear
something positive. Their affirmation tank should
always be full because of you. That's not just for

people whose love language is words of affirmation. That should be true for everyone.

The world has a lot of things that weigh us down. The heaviness of life, in a figurative way, rests upon our shoulders. We bring those things home with us. In a literal way, gravity is what keeps us down. So literally and figuratively our words should include some levity—something that lightens the load, makes us smile, and makes us laugh. Refresh each other's souls with words of encouragement. Metaphysically, your body will thank you. Your stress levels will go down. And all because the person who said "I do" actually seems to still want to. They think you're worth talking to.

Here's the last foundational piece of great communication in marriage:

If you make everything a big deal, then nothing's a big deal!

There are tons of important things in marriage. We've already referenced some of those, but we know there are things that make or break marriages. We also recognize that even if a specific conversation or interaction wouldn't make or break this thing, if we don't address it, it has the potential to become a bigger issue down the road. So, let's talk about it.

But we have to maintain perspective.

Years ago, we heard John Maxwell say, "A person who overreacts in a situation with someone else values that situation more than they value that person."

We'll use an example with our kids to illustrate the larger point.

Imagine my toddler son walked into the living room with a cup of milk in his hand, tripped and fell. The lid came off the cup and milk got all over the floor. In response I immediately screamed at him, "WHAT ARE YOU DOING? DON'T YOU KNOW MILK WILL RUIN CARPET? I CAN'T BELIEVE YOU WOULD BE SO CARELESS AND RUIN OUR FLOORS WITH A FULL CUP OF MILK."

What did I just communicate to my son?

My carpet is more important than you.

Should we correct incorrect behavior? Yes. Are there times when that requires tough conversations and addressing issues within a person that caused a specific behavior? Absolutely. But when we react out of anger and without proper perspective, we are usually communicating something far more serious than whatever they just did.

Closing Thoughts

My (Jeremy) favorite television series of all time is *The West Wing*. I've probably watched the entire series from start to finish five or six times in the 20 years since it first aired. I secretly wanted to run for president of the United States when I was a kid, so a show about the inner workings of the White House and the government is intriguing to me. In one of the final episodes of the series, Danny Concannon is asking CJ Cregg to include him in her thoughts about what will happen after the transition of power when she moves out of the White House. She is baffled and a little offended that he thinks he should have a say in what she would do next. In response he says, "I just want to talk because I like the sound of your voice."

Communication is all the things we've mentioned here. It's listening more than you speak. It's body language and tone and words. It's speaking life and recognizing the power your words hold.

It's also just talking. It's sharing your hopes and dreams with one another. It's staying up late or getting up early to drink a cup of coffee and debrief the day or talk about what's next. It's putting the kids to bed, sitting on the couch, and laughing together as you retell the goofy things they did that day. It's driving in the car with no destination in mind and dreaming about where you want to be in five years.

It's just wanting to talk because you still like the sound of their voice.

HOW TO SHOW LOVE

I (Corrie) don't remember when I first heard the phrase "actions speak louder than words," but it stuck. How often since we were children and were admonished with these words have we repeated them, modeled them, or longed for them?

We've already referenced Gary Chapman's book *The Five Love Languages*, and it is a powerful resource for every couple to consider. The summary is that each of us receives love most effectively in a specific way. The five love languages are **words of affirmation**, **quality time**, **physical touch**, **gifts,** and **acts of service**.

You may already know your love language and that of your spouse. If not, or if it's been a while since you've looked at it, we encourage you to revisit it soon. It doesn't mean you can't connect in more than one way, but there is definitely one predominate way you feel most loved when someone uses that means to engage you.

Acts of service are often overlooked in marriage. Like we did in the last chapter, *words of affirmation* are promoted as part of good communication. *Quality time* is a focus to create shared experiences and maintain health in your relationship. *Physical touch* implies sexual AND non-sexual touch to deepen the intimacy you share with one another. Finally, *gifts* are given and received on birthdays, anniversaries, and other holidays.

But *acts of service* might just be the most important of them all.

Even if it isn't at the top of your list of love languages, when your spouse intentionally does something to serve or help you, it speaks far more than words. It implies they were thinking about you. They know what things stress you out, and they are willing to partner with you in sharing the load.

Galatians 5:13-14 For you were called to freedom, brothers. Only do not use your freedom as an opportunity for the flesh, but through love serve one another. For the whole law is fulfilled in one word: "You shall love your neighbor as yourself."

Serving one another is the easiest way to combat selfishness. We have been given freedom by God to do whatever we want to do in many regards. How should we choose to use that freedom? Not by giving into our flesh and selfishly thinking only about what we desire, what we want to do, or where we want to go. No, we should use the freedom we have to think about someone else and find ways to help them.

One day Jesus was asked, "What is the greatest commandment?" He replied, "Love the Lord your God with all your heart, soul, mind, and strength, and the second is like it, love your neighbor as yourself." In the Galatians passage above, Paul is quoting a portion of that response, where Jesus was quoting from the Old Testament. He reminds us to love our neighbors as much as, and in the same ways, we love ourselves.

We are called to consider others as much as we consider ourselves, and that's tough because we think about ourselves A LOT. If you don't think that's true, next time you take a group picture and then see it for the first time, notice where your eyes go first. To you. How do I look? Is my hair in my face? Did I blink? Oh, who are all those other people in this picture with me?

Beyond group pictures, we often put ourselves first even if we don't say it out loud or fight for what we want. However, in marriage we aren't in this by ourselves. We have someone we committed to love, honor, and cherish. We told them we would care for them in the good times and the bad. So how do we do that?

First, it really does start with communication. Tell each other what you need. How can they help? Saying it out loud doesn't make you needy. We know, you just want them to be able to read your mind. But guess what—they can't! So at least in the beginning, you are going to have to verbally express the things they can do to help you. It's also important to remember that this is a partnership, so it's give and take. Both partners should be looking for ways to serve one another.

Here's a small example. I (Corrie) load the dishwasher. Jeremy unloads the dishwasher. Maybe that seems trivial to you, but in our rhythm it works. I don't mind cleaning up after meals or working throughout the day to put things in. On the flip side, Jeremy is incredibly talented in almost every area of his life, but he couldn't load a dishwasher correctly if he was on a game show and $100,000 was on the line. Somehow, he can't figure out how to get more than four plates and six cups in there. He can pack the luggage for our family of six into a small trunk for a weeklong vacation with no problem, but more than one meal's worth of cutlery trips him up. He's not too proud to ask for help (and he will admit he's watched YouTube videos), but if you throw a pot, pan, or colander at him, he's just going to do two loads. However, first thing in the morning before Jeremy goes to work, he will unload all the dishes, put them away, and leave the dishwasher empty for me to reload throughout the day.

It works for us.

Maybe one of you is better with finances, so you pay all the bills. Or maybe one of you gets stressed by money, so you ask the other to shoulder that load. No matter the social expectations, maybe the wife loves the yard work, or the husband enjoys vacuuming. Find what works for you, talk about it, and then run the play.

Life gets busy. The other night we pulled into the garage and we just stayed in the car. I looked at Jeremy and said, "Hi, I'm Corrie, your wife." Sometimes when things are going crazy, it feels like we're just roommates or co-parents living in the same house. But we are a couple, and we should constantly be looking for ways to show our spouse we love them by helping them with the things they are doing.

This requires you to listen to their needs. Remember listening from the last chapter? Active listening—not thinking of things you are about to ask them to do for you, but intently listening to what they are saying. Even when it isn't the subject of the conversation you're in at that moment, what things stress them out? What tasks are they constantly complaining about? After you hear them say these things out loud, ask, "Is that something I could do for you?" or "Would it help you if I helped with that for a while?" If you've never asked a question like that before, you might see all the blood drain from their face. But if it's presented sincerely, you're going to see a weight lifted and a deep sense of appreciation. The longer you're together the more you can anticipate these things, but don't assume they know what you need or that you are willing to help. Just talk about it.

Closing Thoughts

So often when this subject comes up, we think of it as "tasks." We better do the dishes, take the kids to practice, pay the bills, or help clean the house. It absolutely could be some or all those things, but those are just the actions that communicate something much larger.

When we DO something FOR our spouse, we are actually SAYING something TO our spouse.

"I'm thinking about you" and "I value you." It just requires some intentionality and humility. Maybe before you move on to the next chapter, you can take a few minutes to think about your spouse. What could you do that would relieve some of their stress? What's the one thing you could do today that would communicate your love to them most effectively?

Now go do it.

Fri-Dates

Do you remember when you first started dating? You wanted to be together as much as humanly possible. You would rearrange your whole world to spend just a few minutes together. In the days before cell phones, you would pull the home phone cord as far as it would stretch and lay on your bed talking and then eventually just listening to each other breathe because no one wanted to hang up first.

Does it still feel like that?

If not, why not?

The butterflies in your stomach may not be as active now as they once were, but there should still be a desire to spend time together and the effort to make it happen.

What we discovered pretty early on in marriage is that each of us needs different things to feel connected to one another. This isn't about communication and sex; we address those elsewhere. This is specifically about the way we feel connected in the times that we're together.

Jeremy is a "quality time" person. If we are together, he wants it to feel special. He wants to make sure we cut out the distractions and focus on one another. Corrie is a "quantity time" person. It doesn't really matter what's happening as long as we're together. So, while Corrie is making dinner, Jeremy is sitting in the kitchen, and the kids are running in and out, and the oven timer is going off, and the dryer is buzzing that it's done, and Alexa is making an announcement…it still feels like a win for Corrie because we're together. Jeremy, not so much. That feels like chaos.

We have to be intentional to make sure each of us gets the kind of time that refills our tanks. There are lots of moments when we are just in the same vicinity of one another, doing life, and creating "quantity time" for Corrie. We are also intentional to create space for dedicated "quality time" with one another for Jeremy. No matter which one of us you most identify with, we all need both quantity and quality time. It's not either/or, it's both.

So how do we do it, and how can you?

When our kids were very young, we decided that regular date nights out were difficult to pull off. We didn't have family that lived close, so it required someone else to babysit. Sometimes we couldn't afford it, other times it was a lot of work to get the kids settled and the babysitter to the house for just enough time to grab a quick dinner and a movie. So, we started doing regular "date nights in." These took a lot of different forms, but it might be:

- Getting the kids to bed and laying down to watch a movie without distraction
- Cooking a meal or doing a project together
- Ordering pizza and eating it in bed
- or so many other things.

We still went out on dates, but we tried to add free/cheap/quick/easy things to prioritize time together.

Once the kids all started school, we leveraged Jeremy's off day: Friday. We started taking "Fri-Dates."
- Lunch and a matinee before school pick up
- Something for both of us such as Top Golf and Target
- Driving toward the mountains to do some antiquing or just looking at the scenery and houses as we drive and dream about the future

Sometimes it costs money, and other times it is just the investment of time.

Then in recent years, we have tried to be very intentional to prioritize at least one trip a year without kids, whether it's just the two of us or with other couples. We say "tried" because we haven't been successful every year, but by talking about it, planning for it, budgeting for it, and blocking off the calendar, we've been successful more years than not. Some examples have been a cruise (secrets on how to do it cheap in a minute), an all-inclusive with friends, quick trips to do something fun, or adding a day or two on the front or back of a work trip.

We've used websites like VacationsToGo.com to book last minute cruises within 90 days if our schedule was flexible. We've used travel agents to help us maximize the money we had to find the best location depending on the deals available or time of year. We've coordinated with friends so we could have shared experiences, and we've leveraged credit card points, SkyMiles, and other benefits to expand what may be possible in the time or on the budget that we've had available.

Obviously, we recognize not everyone has Friday off, so Fri-Dates may not work for you. We also know, depending on your season of life, a vacation without the kids may not be feasible. The specifics are actually less important than the rationale.

How are you choosing to intentionally create time with one another?

Some couples go to the Farmer's Market on Saturday mornings. We've had friends who work out a partnership with another couple in their church or on their street and they swap free childcare. Couple A will watch all the kids while Couple B gets a date night without having to worry about paying for childcare. At some point this week or next Couple B will watch all the kids while Couple A goes out. There are families within our church who use the youth group or kids ministry midweek programming as a 60- to 90-minute window for a date. While that isn't the intended vision for those ministries, if it is the best time for those couples, we are all for it!

Get creative. Ask other couples what they do. Google it. Remember, what you do isn't nearly as important as the fact that you are doing it.

As a pastor, one of my (Jeremy) favorite things to do is go on a trip with our staff. We try to take an annual staff retreat or attend a conference together. There are obvious benefits like increased knowledge and refueling for our souls. There are also secondary benefits. The trip to and from creates amazing moments for conversation. The time spent around the table at meals gives us opportunities to debrief what we're learning. Perhaps my favorite secondary benefit is inside jokes. Trips create space for stories to be shared or things to be done that we can reference when we get back home, and the people who went on the trip are the only ones who know why it's funny.

Now let's bring that into our marriage. How many of the stories you tell about your relationship are from when you were dating? Those were the days we went hiking, to movies and ballgames. Often once we get married, or a few years in, we stop creating memories and inside jokes with each other.

We try to make sure this isn't the case in our marriage. We could tell you hundreds of stories of crazy things we've done just because we wanted to experience something together.

One year our trip away was a cruise, leaving from Los Angeles. We live near Atlanta, so that's not super close, but we cashed in some airline miles, flew out a day early and rented a car to take in all the sights before hopping on the ship. It was Memorial Day weekend at the end of May, which is very warm where we live. As we headed out to the Pacific, we discovered it's pretty chilly on the water that time of year. At our first port we headed straight to a shop to buy Corrie a sweatshirt. She lived in that sweatshirt the rest of the trip.

One of our ports was Ensenada, Mexico. We decided we wanted to do something fun, but we hadn't pre-booked any excursions. So, I (Jeremy) assured Corrie it would be a great idea for us to rent a scooter and drive around. She agreed and we stopped at the first rental shop we could find. While the gentleman was taking our information, I asked him where we could go for a fun experience. He quickly said, "*La Bufadora*." I didn't have my Spanish-English dictionary with me so I wasn't entirely sure what we were getting into, but at this point I was committed. He had my credit card. He explained through our language differences that it should only take me 15 minutes to get there.

Now might be a good time to tell you I had never driven a scooter, and I was unaware that approximately half a mile from the cruise port you left the tourist area and entered a five-lane highway that rivals Atlanta's I-285. We were in rush hour traffic. I wasn't driving along the vacation route. I was driving between 18-wheel semi-trucks. It would also be a good time to tell you that somewhere between his Spanish and my English, 15 minutes was actually 42 kilometers at 55 km/hr. We drove nearly an hour. There were several times Corrie asked me to turn around, but we had paid for this scooter and my man told me *La Bufadora* was beautiful. I wanted to take my bride to see it.

Have I mentioned that *La Bufadora* is loosely translated as "The Blowhole" or "The Snorter?" It's a place in the coastal rocks where the waves hit and throw water high in the air. After 42 kilometers it was a little underwhelming.

We grabbed a few pictures and got back on our scooter to head back to the interstate. It was a long ride back and we didn't want to miss our boat.

I (Corrie) was pretty frustrated riding on the back of that scooter all the way up to that hole. It was unsafe. A rock flew off the tires of the trucks and cut my eye under this helmet that wasn't intended for its current use. It scared me to death. Jeremy nearly missed a stop sign but saw it just in time to slam on the brakes and nearly throw us on the ground. We got wet at *La Bufadora* and snapped a few pictures, but something shifted when we got back on the scooter. I wasn't scared anymore, so I wasn't frustrated anymore. I knew where we were going. I got tickled thinking about telling this story to our friends. We laughed almost the entire 42 kilometers back to the ship. There was also a little market where I got to do one of my favorite things: shop, and Jeremy got to do one of his favorite things: negotiate in open air markets.

That meant we had gifts to carry back on our scooter that was barely big enough for the two of us but, given my frustration on the way out to the hole, I don't think Jeremy would have told me no about anything.

That was also the trip where two drunk ladies on a "divorce-aversary" found out Jeremy was a pastor, sobered up pretty quickly and one of them cried telling us the mistakes she'd made in her marriage. Later they asked Jeremy to baptize them in the hot tub, which he did. If it sounds crazy it's because it was. But it's a story we tell because it happened to us…together.

We're all for each person living their individual lives and creating fun memories alone, with friends, or with their kids. We are also big fans of married couples finding ways to play hide and seek in Target or race each other to the mailbox or ride a scooter together in Mexico.

We aren't big fans of husbands and wives creating all their best memories away from each other. The husband lives his life. The wife lives hers. They spend as much or more time apart as they do together. Most of their new memories and experiences are shared with others. At first this isn't that big of a deal—there's just a little sliver of their lives that are separate. However, the longer they go the larger and larger that divide gets until they find themselves far apart and aren't sure how they got here.

It's not really about experiences or memories, it's about time and togetherness.

Closing Thoughts

There have been seasons in recent years where we started to feel disconnected from one another. Not in a "things are broken, oh no, what are we going to do" kind of way. More like a "I feel like we are the most amazing roommates who really like each other but miss each other" kind of way. Almost every time it can be traced to one of three things: We haven't been on a Fri-Date or a trip together in a while, we haven't had sex recently enough, or we aren't communicating more than just the logistics of our family life. The cool thing is that these start to build on one another. When we prioritize our Fri-Dates, we talk about things that matter, which usually makes us want to get the kids to bed earlier, lock the door and "discuss the budget."

Whether it is a Fri-Date, an all-inclusive resort, or a trip to Taco Bell while the kids are at Vacation Bible School, what are you doing to communicate to your spouse:

"I'm willing to do whatever it takes to spend time with you."

FRIENDS

Ross. Chandler. Monica. Rachel. Phoebe. Joey. For 10 years the world watched as this group of six young adults figured out how to do life, work jobs (sometimes), drink coffee, date, and be friends. More than 52 million people watched the series finale on May 6, 2004. Whether you can quote every episode or you're more of an *Andy Griffith* fan, there's no denying the power of friendship. Like the show *Cheers* before it, *Friends* made us believe that life was better when lived around people who knew your name and loved you at your worst.

Hopefully your life has been filled with meaningful relationships. It is our sincere hope that you have one or more best friends and a lot of good friends. That shouldn't change when you get married.

One of the funniest episodes of the show *King of Queens* is when Doug and Carrie are trying to find new couple friends. One or the other of them doesn't like something about the prospects. If Doug likes them, Carrie hates the wife, and vice versa. It's tough to find couple friends that both of you like, but it's so worth it.

Jim Rohn famously said, "You are the average of your five closest relationships." John Maxwell and others have expounded on that idea and said, "Show me your five closest friends and I'll show you your future." We believe the same can be said for marriage. Show us the five couples closest to you and we can often guess the health of your marriage.

It's tougher to be happily, healthily married if ALL of your couple friends are getting divorced or living in unhealthy relationships. It's not impossible, and you ultimately determine the health of your own marriage, but it absolutely makes it harder to get marriage advice and talk about growing in marriage if you are constantly surrounded by people who are living a different story. The opposite is also true. If you are surrounded by couples who have healthy, growing marriages, it does not guarantee your marriage will be healthy. It does mean you are doing life with people modeling what you want, getting advice from people who have predetermined what success looks like and who have persevered through things like what you're walking through right now.

One of our favorite events at our church is the annual Couple to Couple. The event lasts for four weeks as we gather each Sunday night for a month. We sit around tables with three other couples, share a meal, and play games. Then each night a couple will share a teaching on a relevant topic for engaged and married couples. Many of the topics in this book have been presented over the years — communication, conflict resolution, parenting, intimacy, and forgiveness. The topics tend to repeat every few years because of the commonality of issues couples are dealing with. Then at the end of the teaching segment, the speakers provide three to five discussion questions for each table to talk about before they go home. Some weeks there are additional questions for each couple to discuss on their own before the next Sunday. It's a powerful event!

Over the years we've said to the hundreds of couples who have attended, "This event allows us to sit around tables and laugh together about what other couples are unfortunately home by themselves crying about." Obviously, we aren't making light of those at home. We are recognizing that there is power in community. When you get around a table and hear another wife talk about the dumb thing her husband did last week, you realize your husband isn't the only frustrating one in the world. When another husband shares in the context of conversation that he wishes his wife slept in something other than flannel PJs all the time, you can laugh knowing that maybe other couples wrestle with the same things you do.

Outside of community and friendship you begin to feel isolated and become convinced you're the only one going through what you're going through. That's just not true!

1 Corinthians 10:13a The temptations in your life are no different from what others experience…

This is my (Jeremy) favorite verse of Scripture. If you kept reading you would see that God is faithful and there is always a way out of any temptation you might face. However, my favorite part of my favorite verse is right there at the beginning. "The temptations in your life are no different from what others experience…" It's so easy to believe we are the only ones going through what we're going through. It's easy to convince ourselves no one can relate to what we argue about, but there is a commonality in life AND in marriage that should be comforting. Your brother and sister-in-law might not be going through the same thing you are but a couple in your church probably is. Your best friends may not fight about the exact same things you do but your next-door neighbors probably do.

I (Corrie) remember going to the wedding shower of a college friend after Jeremy and I had been married about six months. Of the girls in attendance, probably half of us were married. At some point I overheard one of the married girls across the room say, "It's unlike anything I've ever seen. All he wants to do is have sex. ALL THE TIME!" Another girl said, "mine too," while the other married girls nodded in agreement. I couldn't help but laugh out loud. I said, "So it's not just Jeremy?" It was soon confirmed that all of our husbands seemed to really like having sex with us.

This led to a conversation about different sex drives that included lots of laughter but also lots of personal reassurance. Up to that point it wasn't that it was a problem, but as I said in the introduction, I grew up in a house of four women. While I had a lot of guy friends growing up, and I had dated several guys before Jeremy and I got married, I wasn't really privy to the inner workings of the male mind. I just could not wrap my head around the persistence of Jeremy's "cardio of choice." I, too, enjoy working out, but was there something wrong that I didn't feel the need to go to the gym quite as often?

To hear other women share that this was common in their relationships made it seem a little more normal. I left the wedding shower that day with a newfound appreciation for my husband, our marriage, and my friends.

All this talk about friendship isn't to imply that you can be friends only with other couples. Just as each spouse needs their own hobbies, passions, and dreams, each individual needs other relationships outside of marriage too.

Ultimately, you decide together what this looks like. Don't feel the pressure to mimic what you see in other couples. If you don't need or want a girl's weekend away twice a year, that's okay. If you really would rather hang out with your wife than the guys most nights, don't feel guilty about that. However, you also shouldn't feel guilty if the two of you determine that creating space for each other to spend chunks of time with others is the healthiest thing for your marriage.

Some of these relationships can just be fun relationships. Golf outings. Shopping trips. Mommy & Me play date groups. Those are great. They provide an outlet for you to decompress from work or connect with people at the same stage of life. There are also relationships that fulfill specific purposes in your life.

Years ago, I (Jeremy) heard a pastor talk about the three relationships everyone needed in their life. I've never forgotten it, and I regularly evaluate my relationships to determine where I'm strong and perhaps where I'm lacking. He said, "Everyone needs a Paul, a Timothy, and a Barnabus."

If you aren't familiar with the reference, these three names come from the New Testament. Paul was an apostle who first appears in the book of Acts as he persecutes Christians. He has a powerful conversion story and begins to travel, preaching and teaching in the synagogues and establishing new churches. Many of the books of the New Testament are actually letters written by Paul to churches he had previously established or groups of people he was helping in spiritual formation. Timothy was Paul's young protege and receives encouragement from him as he begins his own ministry. Barnabus was a peer to Paul and accompanied him on some of his missionary journeys as well.

So, you need a:
Paul - a mentor
Timothy - a protege
Barnabus - a peer

On a personal level, maybe the word *mentor* is intimidating so let's redefine it. You need someone who has already traveled the road you're on. Who can you engage to help you with what you're trying to accomplish? Is there someone at work or who used to work in your field that can help you navigate the career decisions you are making? Seek them out. Ask for some time. Buy their lunch and come ready with some questions to glean much needed wisdom. You would probably be surprised at how eager they are to invest in you.

It can be just as overwhelming to talk about a protege. Most of us don't feel like we are ready to have someone following in our footsteps, but take that reframed mentor definition and apply it here. Who might be looking to someone like you because they are on the journey you've already completed? Maybe you've already walked through the early days of homeschooling your kids, so a mom with young school-aged kids trying to figure out curriculum and schedules would find your experience invaluable to her present reality. This relationship is all about adding value to others.

Perhaps the easiest relationship to wrap our minds around is with Barnabus. Peers and friends are a necessary part of life, regardless of our introverted or extroverted nature. We aren't meant to live life in isolation. We were created for community. God said in Genesis 2:18, "It's not good for man to be alone." In Ecclesiastes 4, we read:

"Two are better than one, because they have a good return for their labor: If either of them falls

down, one can help the other up. But pity anyone who falls and has no one to help them up."

Aloneness leaves us vulnerable.

Here's what we've discovered: You need Paul, Timothy, and Barnabus couple friends too. Every couple needs to be on the lookout for a couple or two who is a few steps ahead of them to learn from. They need to be open to those couples who are coming after them, and they need to have some peers who are at a similar stage of life.

I (Corrie) had this mentor relationship with a lady in our church when Jeremy and I first got married. We were newlyweds eight hours away from "home" and family. We were in ministry together for the first time. To top it all off, we found out just a few months into our marriage that we were expecting our first child. It was all a little overwhelming. God knew that, and he sent Paige. Her husband was on staff with Jeremy, and they were older than us. They actually had children in our youth group. However, Paige had the perfect temperament for me. She didn't make little things seem like a big deal. She was a safe place for me to ask my questions. She was a nurse, and there were countless times during pregnancy and as a new mom that I would call to make sure what I was experiencing was normal. She never made me feel dumb or naive. She listened, she responded, she cared. Robbie and Paige, along with our pastor and his wife, were a blessing to us in those early days of our marriage. I am incredibly thankful for Paige's influence on my life, marriage, and parenting in that season. She mentored me, perhaps without even knowing it.

Sometimes that's the way it goes. Other times the relationship takes on a more formal arrangement or the transfer of information can easily be tracked. Either way, we have to make sure we are intentional about seeking out these relationships.

We wouldn't have been able to tell you 10 years ago who our best friends would be today. Even if we tried to answer, we would have been wrong.

We currently have three couples who add enormous value to our lives. We have known each of them for different lengths of time. In at least two of the instances, we knew them for a period of time before we really got close to them, but now we do life with these three couples. We've been able to literally travel the world with them. We have several group texts—one with just the guys, one with just the girls, and one with all eight of us. Each is filled with everything from jokes, to pictures of our kids, to planning the next trip together, to encouragement, to prayer requests, and everything in between. There's no way we could have known how much each of them would mean to us, but now we can't imagine our lives without them. I (Jeremy) am a better husband because of these men and their wives. I (Corrie) am a better wife because of these women and their husbands. We love them all so much and we desire for every couple we know to have meaningful connections like we have with these friends.

Closing Thoughts

Some people are in your life for a **reason**. You met them on the first day at your new job, and for a while they were your only friend at work. They were the first couple you met when you started attending your new church and weren't sure where to check in the kids. At some point the relationship lessened and you don't talk much anymore, but in the early days they were invaluable to you. Other people are in your life for a **season**. There might not be well-defined start and stop dates, but looking back they were a huge part of your life for a specific period of time. Maybe your kids played on the same team several seasons in a row. Maybe they lived next door before one of you moved. However they came into your life, many of your memories from that span of time include them. Finally, some people are in your life for **life**. You don't really know who these people are until the end. That's not intended to be morbid, but it's true.

We need people from each of these three categories. One isn't less important than the other, because they all serve a purpose in the plan of God for your life. So be on the hunt. Don't allow past hurts in relationships to cause you to pull back. You and your spouse should be on the lookout for other couples and individuals to do life with. It's going to be a little bit awkward at first. They don't know all your stories. You aren't quite sure how much time you want to spend with these people. But lean in. It's worth it. In the words of a mentor of ours in a previous season, "We don't have time to start at step one. Just assume step 20. Let's just go all in. We can always go back and fill in the backstory later."

INTIMACY

"I'm on the way home. Meet me in the bedroom."

Those were the words I (Jeremy) heard my wife say on the other end of the phone. I'm glad she didn't say anything really important after that because I wouldn't have heard it.

I (Corrie) will pick up the story from here. What prompted this phone call, you ask? A simple gift certificate. For my birthday one year, Jeremy purchased me a gift card to a salon for a foot massage and reflexology session. I didn't really know what I was getting. We had a friend who had recently gone to this salon, had a great experience, and recommended it to us. I don't know that she had a similar experience to what I'm about to describe. She just said it was a great place and a great massage. So, when it came time for my birthday Jeremy called, paid over the phone, printed out the gift certificate, and presented me with the gift.

A few weeks later I decided to cash in the certificate. I got ready, left the house, and Jeremy stayed back with the kids. Upon my arrival to a very nice building in a nice part of our town, the staff gave me a tour, and then took me to a room with massage chairs, dim lights, and comforting music where I waited. They asked me what blend of oils I would like during my massage. I had no idea, so they handed me a menu of possibilities. Some of the options were for very specific health issues or stressors, but I didn't see one that jumped out, so I just selected a hormone balancing blend.

Over the next hour I received a great massage, including pressure point treatment on parts of my feet and legs, and was pampered by the staff. It was a beautiful gift from Jeremy and the kids, and I was thoroughly enjoying the experience.

Then something happened.

As the massage was ending and they began the pedicure, my body began to respond to the oils or something because I experienced feelings I can't really describe. I've been asked by friends if I thought was drugged, but I definitely don't think so. It felt very natural; it just felt *different*. I needed to get home to Jeremy, and fast.

The pedicure ended. I presented the gift certificate and headed to the car. I knew I was about 20 minutes from the house, so I picked up the phone and gave Jeremy a call.

I (Jeremy) will pick up the story from here. I've spent my children's inheritance ordering various hormone balancing essential oils, but I've yet to find the right one. I'm not giving up!

Wouldn't it be great if sex and intimacy (we'll use those words interchangeably for a few minutes) was like that all the time? Your body and mind working in perfect harmony to create passionate experiences with your spouse on a regular basis. For us, that story was an isolated event. While we have a healthy sex life, it doesn't work like that most of the time. It also doesn't usually work like it does in shows and movies.

There's nothing wrong with that.

Let yourself off the hook if you entered into marriage with preconceived ideas that just didn't turn out that way after "I do." Society has done a terrible job of creating expectations for our sex lives that are almost always unattainable and do more harm than good.

Sometimes this is a result of pornography or cultural pictures of men, women, or sex existing for an individual's instant gratification. Other times it is the result of past hurt or experiences that leave us wounded and vulnerable without a safe place to articulate what we feel. Still other times, this is just the result of assuming that your 16-year-old hormones will still be as active at 30 or 40 and beyond.

Genesis 2:25 "Adam and his wife were both naked, and they felt no shame."

The naked part of your marriage should not invoke shame on either of you. The goal is to live out in the open with each other and feel completely confident while being completely vulnerable. Often these two realities don't coexist. We have vulnerability with insecurity, or we have a false sense of confidence. This reality for Adam and Eve was before sin entered their story in Genesis 3. That can't be said for any of us, so we have to strive to live a God-honoring life in this aspect of our relationship.

We were both virgins on our wedding night. We don't say that as a badge of honor intended to bring guilt or shame on others who may not be able to say that. We say that to offer some context. We had dated other people before dating one another and had experienced varying levels of physical intimacy, but we stood at the altar offering our bodies to one another as a gift never given to another. That didn't lower the expectations of the wedding night and the honeymoon. Surely it was going to be just like the movies and the stories we'd heard.

It was not.

We had to learn to have sex with one another. As much as we just knew we knew what to do, we had to figure some things out. That definitely created some insecurity for both of us, and early on we were not good at talking about sex at all.

The conversation was always awkward. It always felt personally attacking, and it usually happened too close to the moment for one or both of us to be ready to talk about it. But we kept working at it.

While we were engaged, an older husband told us, "Every time you have sex the first year you're married, put a penny in a jar. Every time you have sex after the first year of marriage, take a penny out of the jar. You'll never run out of pennies." The implication is that you'll have sex more in the first year of marriage than you will the rest of your marriage combined. I (Jeremy) immediately told Corrie I wanted to prove that theory wrong. We don't keep score or keep count, but I can safely assume we've run out of pennies.

We talk about this more in a later chapter about stages of marriage, but it's important to remember that you aren't always going to be in sync about when you want to have sex, and that's okay. Each partner has a different sex drive, with different external stressors and other factors that impact mood and desire. We have to be aware of our own tendencies and the patterns of our spouse in order to be fair to one another.

Several years ago, my (Jeremy) brother, Jason, made this statement:

"There will be one week a month where *you* will want to have sex. There will be one week a month where *your spouse* will want to have sex. There will be one week a month where you'll *both* want to have sex. And there will be one week a month where *neither* of you will want to have sex."

Maybe those timelines aren't true in your marriage but if you're honest, I bet there is a natural pattern that has developed in your relationship. Talk about it with one another. Perhaps it needs some tweaking, but it could be that saying it out loud allows you to embrace it and create more realistic expectations of one another.

Expectations are a tricky thing. Often when we get in trouble it's because we have created unspoken, unrealistic expectations for one another. At a marriage conference years ago, a husband shared that early in their marriage he walked through everyday believing that "sex was *on the table* tonight." He wasn't thinking about it all day, but he assumed that tonight they *might* have sex. He never articulated that to his wife. So, on those nights when he was in the mood, he tried to determine if she was too. If he read her body language as "It's probably not going to happen," he went to bed frustrated. Not just sexually frustrated—relationally frustrated. Ultimately, he was upset with his wife because she didn't know he wanted to have sex.

How often do we do that? We get angry or, at the very least, frustrated because something they didn't even know we were thinking or hoping didn't happen. That's not fair to our partners. You can take it outside the context of sex and put it anywhere else in your marriage. Unspoken expectations almost always go unmet. Just speaking them doesn't insure they will happen, or that they should, but it does get both of you on the same page.

Sex is a gift given by God to the two of you. It wasn't intended to be shared with anyone else. No matter how much the world tries to distort sex and make it something to be explored as freely as you choose, sex was intended for the context of marriage between a husband and a wife. Explore that gift. Enjoy that gift. Give lots of grace to your intimacy partner.

Intimacy. That's a word we don't use a lot. It is used but often interchangeably with other words, as we have done in this chapter, or incorrectly in a variety of contexts.

Miriam-Webster and others define *intimacy* as closeness or a familiarity with one another. The act of sexual intercourse is included in most definitions but is down the list. This should line up with the priorities of intimacy within marriage. Husbands and wives should obviously be having sex with one another, but that should not be the full extent of their intimacy.

1 Corinthians 7:5 Do not deprive one another, except perhaps by agreement for a limited time, that you may devote yourselves to prayer; but then come   together again, so that Satan may not tempt you because of your lack of self-control.

This entire section of 1 Corinthians 7 responds to questions about sex within marriage. There's a component of mutual submission to one another spelled out here. Husbands and wives have given themselves to one another and, as such, should use their bodies to serve one another. The caveat is that they can abstain for a time for spiritual reasons. However, that abstention shouldn't last so long that it causes spiritual consequences. The implication is that sex is an important part of the marital relationship, but it isn't the only part of the relationship.

While a healthy sex life can create greater intimacy, we should start from a place of intimacy with one another that leads to a healthy and fulfilling sex life.

The word intimacy is somewhat self-defining.

IN-TO-ME-SEE

An intimate relationship is one where you give the other person access to all of you. This is why sex plays such an important role—you are physically giving yourself to one another. However, there are at least three other aspects to intimacy: mental, emotional, and spiritual.

Our friends Dave and Ashley Willis are an incredible resource for married couples. They host *The Naked Marriage* Podcast and speak at XO Marriage events throughout the country. They challenge couples to be "mentally monogamous." It's not enough just to be physically monogamous and not give yourself physically to someone else. You must also keep your mind committed. This includes not filling your mind with other thoughts, images, or conversations with people who are not your spouse. Your thought life drives so much of your behaviors in life and marriage.

Does your spouse have access to your mind? Do they know your thoughts? Do they know the crazy things you think about? If not, why not? Not everyone in your life needs to know your thoughts, but someone does. Why not give your spouse access to your mind? This kind of mental intimacy says to your partner, "You get access to all of me, even the crazy, random thoughts I have sometimes because they are part of who I am. I don't want to just give you the filtered version of me, I want you to see all of me." That's a powerful declaration.

Emotional intimacy is similar. You are giving your spouse access to your emotional being — happiness, sadness, fears, anxieties and so much more. If they only have access to your external responses, they are always playing catch up. They can't respond until you've reacted out of your emotions. However, if you open up in emotional intimacy to grant them access on the front end, they can help you in advance to process in healthier ways. You become teammates and partners in your effort to be fully transparent with one another.

Lastly is spiritual intimacy. This doesn't just apply to Christians. We believe that every person is a spiritual being having a human experience and not the other way around. James 4:5 says, "He jealously desires the spirit He placed inside of you." Meaning that even prior to someone being in a relationship with Jesus, He is in pursuit of a relationship with your spirit. You have a past, a story, hurts and pains, successes, and dreams. You put your faith in something. Open up to your spouse and give them access to the spiritual side of you.

What happens if you don't do some of these things? You begin to have secrets from your spouse. There are things you feel, think, and do that they don't know about. That becomes dangerous. Dave and Ashley also remind us "Secrecy is the enemy to intimacy."

Not every secret will break a marriage, but a pattern of secrecy will.

When a husband starts keeping things from his wife and she finds out, she begins to wonder what else he might be hiding. When a wife isn't open and honest with her husband and he finds out, he begins to doubt if he can trust her in other areas. Never convince yourself "no one will ever find out." There are too many stories that reveal the opposite reality for you to believe this lie. Give your spouse access to every part of you, even the smallest details.

Song of Solomon 2:15 says "catch for us the foxes, the little foxes that spoil the vineyards."

It's those little foxes, those little secrets, those little pieces you don't share with your spouse that spoil the vineyard of intimacy in your marriage.

Let's commit to being intimate with our spouse in every part of our lives. When intimacy increases, so will our level of connection, satisfaction, and fulfillment. We don't have a stat to back it up, but we're willing to stake our reputations on this reality: When you both commit to living more intimate lives, you will find more satisfaction in the bedroom.

It's not our intent to minimize issues you may be facing in your marriage related to intimacy and sex. There are very real issues couples face and a few pages in this book won't solve all of those issues. We encourage you to talk about whatever issues exist in this area of your relationship. Often a pastor or professional counselor can help make sure you are talking about the right things to bring about healing here. It's important, so don't stop working on it.

While you should keep talking about it, one word of caution is be careful who you talk about it with. Maybe you have a best friend or confidant that you tell everything. This subject may not need to be included in your conversations. As we've already mentioned, sex and intimacy create incredible vulnerability. The last thing you want to do is have your spouse find out you are talking about issues in this area with other people, especially if you aren't talking with each other about it. That could create enormous insecurity in them. So, start by talking about it with one another and, if necessary, engage a professional.

Our desire is for you to find fulfillment in this area of your life. Intimacy looks a little different in every relationship, and your sex life is dependent on a number of factors. However, we think there are a few final thoughts that will help every couple.

First, sex starts in the driveway. We know, other people say it starts in the kitchen, and it can start there too. It can also start in the hallway, the garage, at work, on the phone, and in the car. Really, it starts anywhere you want it to start. However, it rarely starts between the sheets.

Whether the act of sex takes two minutes or two hours, the build up to sex could take several hours or even several days. The way you communicate with one another first thing in the morning sets the tone. The texts you send throughout the day could set the mood. The way you listen and respond during dinner keeps the ball rolling.

Maybe you've heard the phrase "men are microwaves, women are crockpots." That's obviously a very cliche, gender-based stereotype that may not be true in your marriage. And yet, we have rarely seen two microwaves or two crockpots married to one another. So, you have to be aware of who you are and who your spouse is.

If you're married to a crockpot, you can't expect them to be ready to go at a moment's notice, with the kids still awake, while the dishes are in the sink, and a million other things are going on. They need time to eliminate distractions, get their mind engaged, and make sure they can be fully present. If you're married to a microwave, be careful with your words. If you say, allude to, hint at, or wink-wink nudge-nudge and then nothing happens, they may get frustrated. Neither appliance is the right or only way to approach sex, and sometimes crockpots want to microwave and sometimes microwaves need to crockpot. But by knowing who you are and who they are, you'll approach sex in a more fulfilling way.

If any part of that illustration makes you smile, giggle, or even laugh out loud, that's fantastic. The second principle is: We are big believers in finding the humor in our sex lives. We are sharing a part of our lives with each other that no one else gets access to. So sometimes it is HOT! Sometimes it is very romantic. Sometimes it's quick. And sometimes it's funny.

One of our favorite family and small group games is Catchphrase. If you've never played the game, you hold a digital device in your hand, click start, and a word appears on the screen. You have to describe that word while your partners attempt to guess correctly before the timer runs out. One time my (Jeremy) brother, Jason, was playing, and after reading the word to himself, he started to say the word and stammered and stuttered for a few seconds before he yelled, "WHEN YOU HAVE SEX REAL FAST!" Those types of clues and words don't usually appear in this game so it took us a second, but someone finally yelled out "quickie" and Jason said yes as he passed the device to the next person—his wife, Andrea. She looked at the screen and immediately handed it back and said, "That word is quiche, like the food." If you don't think Corrie and I have used the word *quiche* as a code word to set a meeting with each other, you're crazy.

Sometimes you just have to laugh!

Closing Thoughts

Intimacy is not just sex, but sex should be very intimate. Even when it's funny. Even when it's a quiche. As we've already stated, you are sharing a part of yourself with your spouse that no one else in the world gets access to. Enjoy that. Get good at it. Talk about it. Have sex as much as one or both of you desires to do so and give and receive tons of grace in the process.

**Your SEXUAL DESIRE should only be
for your SPOUSE.**

**Your SPOUSE should not only be
for your SEXUAL DESIRE.**

Go back and read that again. Your sexual desire should be reserved only for your spouse. Don't allow your eyes, ears, or mind to place desire on anyone else. At the same time, don't view your spouse as only for your sexual pleasure. They are far more than that. When we isolate this one part of our relationship, we are missing the fullness of the gift they are to us.

The world we live in has equally elevated and devalued sex at the same time. They have elevated it to be prominent in nearly every television show, movie, book, and advertising campaign. It seems to be everywhere you turn. This has devalued what sex is really all about. Sex was intended to be a gift between a husband and a wife to be fully enjoyed within the context of marriage. As sex has continued to find its way into other relationships and other arenas of our lives, the level of intimacy we often share with one another has decreased. This is heartbreaking.

Fight for greater intimacy. Be open and honest with every area of your life. Seek to understand, and watch your emotional, mental, spiritual, and physical intimacy increase in exponential ways.

RESOLVING CONFLICT

Do you remember the tug of war from gym class or church camp as a kid? It was intense. Usually, it involved very strategic decisions in advance. Put the big kid in the loop at the back, scatter the other kids, and put a strong kid or two near the front. It also involved a lot of yelling once the whistle blew. You had to pull with all your might to get the bandana in the middle over to your side. However, this was rarely the end of the match. Usually, the match ended when all of the kids on the other side of the rope came tumbling to your side because you had overpowered and outlasted them. The losers might land on people, end up with bruises, or get serious rope burn from the final pull. The winners rarely escaped injury free. They, too, might have rope burn, little splinters from cheap or old ropes, and muscle aches from pulling so hard for so long.

Unfortunately, in marriage this is the image that so often comes to mind when we think about serious conflict. Not the kind of conflict where we can't decide what we want for dinner. We're talking about the kind of conflict that raises the volume in the room, adds red to the cheeks, and causes the dog to hide under the bed.

I'm pulling on one side. You're pulling on the other side. May the best man or woman win.

We pull out all our ammo from past arguments and the history of our time together. "You always...," "You never...," "You promised me...," and so much more. We pull as hard as we can for as long as we can until the other side gives in, and we win this battle.

Unfortunately, that's not only unhealthy long term, it's not even the right picture of what we are as a couple. We aren't on opposite sides of the rope pulling against each other. We are on the same side of the rope, on the same team, pulling against the various other pressures coming against us.

Obviously, there are serious issues that need in-depth and serious conversations. There are problems that may need a counselor to help you sort through. There are hurts that can't be healed overnight. None of what we are saying negates those realities. However, outside of abuse and patterns of unfaithfulness, almost every situation should be given ample time and opportunities to navigate toward a solution.

Previously, when talking about *communication* we referenced one of the guiding principles of our marriage: If you make everything a big deal, then nothing's a big deal. When something is a big deal, it needs to be made a big deal and handled with the kind of seriousness and sensitivity warranted. But how many little things have we made the equivalent of World War III?

We recently talked to an older couple who has been married over 50 years. We love those conversations as we have a chance to pick the brain of fellow sojourners so much farther down life's path. We asked them what we ask a lot of couples: "What's the secret to having a healthy marriage for so long?" The wife replied, "Kiss each other on the lips every day." The husband replied, "Don't fight about stupid stuff." We thought both answers were amazing, so we asked them to expound on each. The wife continued her thought by saying, "Kissing is special. When you kiss every day, you remember who you fell in love with." The husband continued his thoughts by saying, "When you get our age, you really have to decide if you want to work up the energy to fight about something you won't really remember fighting about in a few weeks anyway."

When I (Jeremy) was in college, I had a friend who used the "10-Year Rule" filter. He would say, "If you'll remember it in 10 years, it's worth doing." Looking back that's a horrible strategy for life, but at 18 it sounded like a great way to do a lot of fun things.

What if we tweaked the 10-year rule and applied it to our conflict? If this argument won't matter in 10 weeks, let's not argue about it! Obviously, there are some holes in the theory, but we think you understand where we are going. Let's quit arguing about things that don't really matter.

Romans 12:18 If it is possible, as far as it depends on you, live at peace with everyone.

To live at peace with everyone, you have to figure out how to live at peace with the one who sleeps in your bedroom. Notice it doesn't say, "as far as it depends on them." It says, "as far as it depends on you." I can only be accountable for my part in our conflict.

I (Corrie) am an Enneagram 9. Over the years in our marriage and ministry, we've used a variety of personality assessments to understand ourselves and our staff better. What makes me tick? How do you like to receive information? How quickly are you comfortable giving critique to an idea? It's all really helpful. The Enneagram has been one of those we've used, and the number 9 is called "The Peacemaker." When I heard that phrase and began to read about it years ago, it put language to things I had struggled to communicate literally my whole life. I won't go into all the details, but as a middle child I often deferred to others, not speaking up to share my opinion or rebut something someone else said, even if I believed I was right.

When I was a teenager, our church youth group had a lock-in and during one of the games I fell very hard on my shoulder and immediately thought I had broken my arm. The leaders were convinced it wasn't broken, even asking me to lift my arm up over my head. I lifted my arm and thought I was going to black out. They let me lie down, but I was in excruciating pain. The next morning, I got back to my mom and she took me to the emergency room where an X-ray confirmed my arm was in fact broken. They also noted that my blood pressure was extremely high from the pain, and I finally got the first dose of medicine. While everyone involved could have handled the situation differently, looking back I have to take some of the responsibility because I didn't speak up. I didn't communicate clearly that I knew my arm was broken. I needed medicine. I needed my mom. I just stayed quiet and compliant because I didn't want to be a bother to the leaders or disrupt the event.

Some of you cannot relate to that at all, while others have probably done similar things to keep the peace. In our marriage this has been a pattern. I'm really laid back. There aren't many things that bother me. Ninety-nine percent of the time, I'm cool, calm, and collected.

Until I'm not.

In a very cliché example that we've used for years at marriage conferences, on a random Tuesday Jeremy will leave his coffee cup *next to* the sink. Not in the sink. Not in the dishwasher. Next to. It's possible, even probable, that he's done this 100 times in the last 100 days. Each of the last 99 times I was fine. Eventually, I grabbed it, rinsed it out, and put it in the dishwasher. I didn't even mention it to him because it didn't bother me. Until today.

Today it bothers me. And it bothered me for the last 100 days. And I need him to know I'm bothered by it. So, I just keep communicating my bothered-ness until he knows just how bothered I am.

We've been married long enough now that I need to recognize my triggers. Even if day 37 doesn't make me angry, I could do a better job communicating my potential frustration, or even my thoughts about the sharing of household tasks so it doesn't fester on the inside of me.

Another thing I know is that once I'm angry I just need some time to process. I don't want to talk it out right now. I don't have all the words formed in my head that I want to say, and if you force me to talk about it right now, I'm probably going to say some things I later regret. I can't wait indefinitely, and I know that, but I need "a minute" before we can resolve it.

I (Jeremy) have somewhat the opposite problem. I want to resolve any tension that exists between us right now. Even when I'm not entirely sure what the totality of the issue is. I'm almost always the first one to apologize, but it's usually too quick. I don't mean to contradict Scripture about resolving anger quickly, but you have to at least understand what's upsetting the other person before you try to resolve it.

Early in our marriage Corrie and I were discussing something that had created some tension. Until the conversation started, I wasn't actually aware she was frustrated, but before she was even done talking about it I said, "I'm sorry." She looked at me and asked, "For what?" I immediately responded, "I'm sorry for whatever you're upset about."

I could literally write a whole other book on dumb things I've said and done in marriage. Corrie is a saint!

I was apologizing but making it her fault. An apology that starts "I'm sorry you…" isn't an apology. "I'm sorry I…" is the only way to truly own your part of the issue. Even if you aren't 100 percent responsible for the entire issue, and you rarely will be, you are 100 percent responsible for your part. Does that make sense? If I'm only 40 percent responsible for the thing that caused tension in our marriage, I have to own 100 percent of my 40 percent! I can't apologize about my part in this if I don't fully understand how what I did made the other person feel. So, I have to listen. I need to ask questions. I need to process and evaluate what I did and how I could have done it differently, and then I need to apologize as sincerely as I can.

When we first got married and began to have our first arguments and disagreements, we quickly saw our two personalities come out. There is no such thing as a marriage with no conflict. No matter how much you hold your tongue or keep it inside, we are two different people, with two different personalities, influenced by two different families of origin, trying to figure out how to do life together. So, we should have conflict as we attempt to understand one another better and find a middle ground that serves both parties well.

Do you want to know one of the dumbest things I (Jeremy) think we ever argued about?

How positive a person I am.

You read that right. We argued about how positive I am. I thought being a positive person was a good thing, but evidently under the right set of circumstances being positive can be a negative. I am not a "glass half full" guy. I'm a "glass is all the way full. It's half water and half air" guy. I can find a silver lining in nearly every situation. Evidently there were times in our conversations where Corrie just wanted to vent her frustration about something. She didn't need to me to assure her that things weren't that bad, or that the other person probably didn't mean it that way. She didn't need me to be positive. She just needed me to be quiet.

You're going to argue about dumb things. You are also going to argue about very serious things. The goal is to find the best solution for both of you and anyone else involved. This is why it is so important to make sure you stay in the present and don't take a stroll down memory lane. Arguments that include a history lesson aren't always productive. We have a phrase we use for this:

Fight Fair.

When we are discussing something and it rises to the level of becoming an argument, we have to ensure that we stay focused on what got us here and how we can resolve it. Where we get in trouble is when we derail our conversation about the coffee cup, and we begin using phrases like "you NEVER help me with household chores" or "ALL you ever do is gripe at me about what I'm doing wrong." No matter how bad things are, it's nearly impossible to believe that your spouse has literally NEVER helped you with tasks around the house. We've never met a husband or wife where ALL the words coming out of their mouth were griping words. Definitive language and exaggerative words often help us prove a point, but they rarely move us closer to resolution.

It's entirely possible that there are patterns of behavior that come up over and over in your marriage. We're all creatures of habit. We tend to do the same things over and over in our lives and that weaves its way into the narratives of our marriages.

When we are arguing and one of us drops into this kind of definitive language, the other will remind us "you aren't fighting fair." This is also true when we lose focus on the problem and begin to attack the other person. You aren't fighting fair. Your jabs at the other person probably don't help move them closer to the necessary compromise, forgiveness, or resolution to fix the problem that started this argument in the first place.

It doesn't take long in marriage for us to fall into patterns of arguing. One might be the initiator. One might be the verbalizer. One might be the apologizer. One might be the yeller. One might be the crier. You get it. We have patterns. Often this is made easier to do because we are arguing about the same things we've always argued about.

When we do premarital counseling with couples, we ask what things they argue about at this stage in their relationship. Many of these sweet, young couples will say things like "Oh, we don't argue," or "She's perfect; there's nothing that bothers me." We smile and nod as I'm sure older couples did to us. However, then we try to dig down beneath that layer to find those things that do create tension in their relationship. His family. Her friends. Her work schedule. His bad habits.

Eventually, at least a few things surface. It's at this point that we try to help them be aware of this reality: What you fight about early, you'll probably fight about forever.

Work schedules may change, but the drive to do a job well, at all costs, will probably come up over and over again. The arguments in the future may be about coming home when you said you would, but they come from the same motivating factors. You may move out of your parents' house, but your inability to tell them no is going to create tension in your marriage until you learn how to do that. The argument may be about their unannounced weekend visit or where we spend Christmas, but the underlying issue is the same.

The sooner you get to the place where you can push past *what* you're arguing about and really try to understand *why* you're arguing about it, the sooner you can resolve the actual conflict. It's rare that you are actually fighting about schedules and kids and money and life at home. You are almost always arguing about control, security, respect, affection, or fear.

Closing Thoughts

You want to have a fun conversation? Ask your significant other when the last argument you had was, and what it was about. That's probably going to start another one.

Ephesians 4:26 Be angry and do not sin; do not let the sun go down on your anger.

Anger isn't the problem, nor is it a sin. Unresolved anger is the problem. The only thing worse than conflict is fake peace. The kind of peace that isn't real because we just aren't talking about the stuff that matters. So, when there are things that matter, issues that need to be addressed, even if they are hard conversations, let's resolve them as quickly as we can. We aren't fighting WITH one another; we are fighting FOR one another. We are trying to find a compromise that addresses the issues, moves us both toward the middle (each other), and allows us to move forward more united than ever before.

STAGES IN MARRIAGE

When Corrie and I (Jeremy) met, I was wearing Old Navy carpenter jeans. You know, the kind with the hammer hook on one leg. The thing was, I have never used a hammer on a regular enough basis to need dedicated attire for one. Not to mention that these were the days before skinny jeans, or slim fit, or flex fit, so the legs of those jeans had enough denim to smuggle televisions out of electronics stores.

I'm not the same person I was when we first met. I'm not the same person I was when we got married. Neither is Corrie. I'm so thankful for both of those truths. We should be growing, changing, adapting, learning, and maturing. The differentiator for healthy couples is they are doing those things together. Both partners are becoming the person they are becoming... together.

Comedian Dustin Nickerson says (our paraphrase), "My wife and I are so old now that we snicker during the vows at weddings. Because that's not a marriage. That's a wedding. The next day at the airport when she gets to security and says, 'I forgot my passport.' That's a marriage."

One of our favorite marriage stories happened at the airport just a few hours into us even being married. To set up the story you need to know that as the groomsmen in our wedding were walking down the aisle, each shook my (Jeremy) hand, and each included a condom in that handshake. So, while standing at the front of Corrie's home church with friends and family staring at me, I was trying to hide condoms in my pocket. After the ceremony the families were gathered for pictures while everyone else was waiting in the reception. The groomsmen decided now would be the time to play another little trick on me, so they sent our six-year-old nephew up with a pair of fuzzy handcuffs. My "holiness" grandparents were standing very close, so I immediately grabbed them and stuck those in my pocket as well.

The remainder of the evening went off without incident, and when it came time for the sendoff, we got in the limo and started to drive away. However, the items in my pockets of the thin, rented tuxedo pants were creating issues, so I took them out and stuck them in the side of Corrie's bag. I didn't think another thing about it until the next day when we were walking through airport security. It's important to note that we got married two years after the events of September 11th. It was actually Corrie's first time flying since then, and she was so diligent to take off her shoes, belt, and put all her liquids in the preapproved containers. In short, she didn't want anything to be an issue. She put her bag through the x-ray machine and walked through the security checkpoint. We waited and waited and waited. Finally, one of the TSA employees asked Corrie, very loudly, "Ma'am is this your bag?" Corrie was mortified and timidly responded, "Yes, it is. What's the problem?" About that time the woman reached for the side zipper, and I just started laughing. She pulled out the fuzzy handcuffs and held them high for the whole world to see. "Are these your handcuffs?" Corrie had seen the guys hand them to me, but had no idea they were in her bag. Part of me just wanted to play along and say, "Corrie, you should have known you needed to put those in your checked bag for our honeymoon!" But I didn't do that to my shy, introverted, red-faced new bride. I explained the situation to the security guard. She showed us how the lock had a safety on it and said they weren't an issue, so we could keep them. Corrie still felt the need to justify them and said, "See, we didn't even know how they worked so obviously they aren't ours and we haven't used them." We were allowed to leave without being detained any further, only to turn around and see my parents' former boss and one of our denominational church leaders standing right in front of us. I'm not sure they knew what happened, but we couldn't ever look them in the eyes after that.

That's a marriage.

Vows are such a vital part of most wedding ceremonies, and we are obviously in favor of them as we've quoted various portions of them throughout this book. However, vows are aspirational. We can't truthfully say, "I will love you for better or worse, for richer or poorer, in sickness and in health, until death parts us," because those things haven't happened yet. Not in the context of our marriage anyway. So, we are promising to do those things whenever they happen in the future. But at 21 or 25 or 30 or 35, how can you really know what you'll do in years

1, 6, 11, or 52 of marriage? So, why are vows important? Because they position us to think about the future. A future that isn't lived out in a straight line. It's a future lived in seasons. Ebbs and flows. Ups and downs. The sincere hope is when I get to each of those seasons, I will be more committed to keeping those vows than I was the day I made them.

With this in mind, we must set realistic expectations for our marriage and for our spouse. We don't lower the bar. Marriage should call us higher. So, we give grace based on the pace and place.

Here is a list of some of the various seasons of marriage. This list isn't exhaustive, but perhaps it contains enough of the common seasons of most marriages that it allows for each of us to see ourselves in proper perspective.

Newlywed Stage

What a fun season! You come home from the honeymoon to setup a home and a life together. There are so many decisions to be made in this season that few people warn you about. No one tells you that whichever side of the bed you choose that first night will be your side of the bed for the rest of your life. That's a lot of pressure.

You've known for a while the things you loved about your spouse. His eyes. Her laugh. His sensitivity. Her work ethic. His love for your family. Her culinary genius. How could you not fall in love? They are perfect.

The newlywed stage is that time where you learn they are not, in fact, perfect. This is the stage where you learn the things you don't love about them. He snores. She grinds her teeth. He is moodier than you knew. She is more judgmental. He falls asleep during movies now. Little stuff.

Big stuff. It's just stuff, but it starts to show up during this season.

This is a great season to continue what you hopefully started while you were engaged: dreaming about the future. Do you want to have kids? If so, how many? Do you want to adopt? Would you be willing to move for work? Where would you love to travel together one day? It's just a dream right now, so nothing is off limits. Be careful not to crush a dream your spouse has because you can't make the details work in your head right now. Sure, they want 12 kids, and you're not sure your body or the budget could sustain that, but we're just dreaming. Let's talk about it. You're allergic to shellfish, but she thinks a scuba diving trip for your 20th anniversary a couple decades from now would be fun. Maybe so. Let's keep talking about it. You aren't being silently agreeable. You are keeping as many options on the table as possible. There will be a lot of things in your life and marriage that will try to rob you of what's possible. Create a safe place for your spouse to dream.

If you find yourself here now, enjoy this season. Do fun things together. Create memories. Pay off debt. Have lots of sex. Learn how to communicate. Someone else chose you, and you chose them. That's powerful!

Baby Season

It doesn't take too long for young couples to start getting the question: "How long are you guys planning to wait to have kids?" People don't mean to meddle in your business. It often seems like the natural next step for most couples. Obviously, there are couples who choose to never have children for a variety of reasons. There are other couples who desperately desire to do so but knowingly, or unknowingly, have physical reasons they can't. Don't let the question frustrate you. Also, don't let the question rush you. You've got to decide what's best for you and not have kids because all of your couple friends are starting to have kids.

We got pregnant with our first pretty quickly. So quickly we had people counting on their fingers how long we'd been married to determine if we'd gotten pregnant before we got married. We did not.

Three months after we got married, I (Corrie) was home one day while Jeremy was working at the church we were serving at in Mobile, AL. He called to tell me the senior adult group's van had broken down on a day trip to Pensacola, so he and another staff member were renting some vans and driving to get them. I mentioned that I had a doctor's appointment and would meet him home later that evening. I thought I was pregnant, but knew if I was, I wasn't very far along. At the doctor's office they did a blood test and confirmed I was a few weeks pregnant. I left, went to the store, and bought a baby bib and a gift bag.

That night when Jeremy got home, I handed him the gift bag. The look on his face was hilarious. He would later say he thought he missed an anniversary or important date and apologized for not having me a gift. He opened the bag, pulled out the baby bib that said "I Love Dad" on it. He laid it to one side and kept digging into the bag. It still hadn't hit him yet. He reached further into the bag and found the home pregnancy test, looked at it, saw the positive result, and his jaw dropped.

I think most women envision the way their husbands will react to big moments. How will he pop the question? How will he react when I say yes? What will he say when he finds out we're pregnant? Well, Jeremy didn't say a word. He stood up calmly and paced up and down the hallway of the rental house where we were living. I don't remember exactly how long it was, but it felt like five minutes. I'm sure it was just 30 seconds or so because the hallway wasn't that long. Eventually, he turned and said, "Are you serious?" I assured him I was. He got the biggest smile on his face, and then he came and hugged me. I think he was in shock!

He was overjoyed. I was too. We had always wanted to have children and now that was going to be a reality. Yes, we had only been married three months, but we believed that God's timing was perfect, and we embraced it. We decided this would be the having babies stage and it was. We had three more children, each about two years apart. At one point we had boys six, four and two years old, and a newborn baby girl. I'm not entirely sure how we did it, but we did, and I wouldn't change it for the world.

We would be crazy not to admit that this season presents specific challenges to your marriage. There are little people living in your house with you now. They might be sleeping in your room, or even your bed. In certain seasons they may have scheduled mealtime access to your wife's breasts.

I (Jeremy) wrote that last line. I remember when Corrie was nursing and after the kids were in bed one night, I decided now might be the right time to escalate our non-sexual cuddling to something else. Corrie, in the sweetest way possible, let out a sigh and said, "Could we not for at least a few minutes? I feel like I've had people hanging off my body all day long." I literally laughed out loud and then I apologized. Then she felt bad. Then I felt bad. It was a whole thing, but eventually we were both laughing. In that moment the season we were in determined the temperature in the room, if you get my drift.

This season requires lots of communication about a lot of things. Your schedules are different as you figure out the sleep patterns of this human who can't talk yet. Finances are different as you run out of the things people gave you at baby showers and start buying diapers and formula and onesies and all kinds of things you never knew you needed. It is imperative that you're intentional about communication in this season.

Husbands, your wife's body has undergone a literal miracle and needs time to recover. One of my biggest pet peeves is when I (Jeremy) hear husbands make jokes or comments about sex during the six weeks after birth. For the record, it might be longer than six weeks, but if you aren't careful you make it sound like your wife only adds value to your life in one way. Don't do that. She might laugh, but don't make her choose to do so. If you need to, talk to her about your needs but don't make her feel guilty.

Final word of encouragement to those who are contemplating having kids for the first time. There's no perfect time to have a kid. Absolutely you should pay off all your debt and save more money and accomplish your work goals and get a little more settled, but if you don't check all the boxes and you both feel like now might be the right time, go for it. Your friends may not understand, your parents may get freaked out, and you may not have all the answers to all the questions the books ask you, but it will be okay.

Millions and millions of people before you had babies and they figured it out. You will too.

School Season

When your kids are in school, there's a whole new set of pressures. The first question you have to answer is where your kids will go to school. In full transparency, all four of our kids went to public school, so that is our context. We have great friends whose kids went to private school, and a number of friends who homeschooled their kids. You have to determine what's best for you and your family.

This is probably the first time in life that your kids are creating experiences that don't involve you. That can be a little unsettling. This is a great time to establish healthy communication patterns in your home and with your kids. The difference in our kids in regard to this is almost cliché. Our three boys would get in the car in the afternoon, and we would ask, "How was your day?" They would respond "good." And that was it. No details. No stories. Nothing. Our daughter was the exact opposite. She skipped to the car and started talking before the door was fully open. We usually knew everything she learned, who was nice and who was mean today, what she had for lunch, and who wore cute outfits.

One of the reasons communication is so important in this season is because you begin to discipline your children. It is very likely you will disagree with your spouse about what and how to discipline your kids. Most marriages include a rule-keeper and a grace-giver, and that's a good thing. Be on the same page as much as possible in advance of correcting your children. When you aren't, don't argue about it in front of your children.

This isn't a parenting book (hopefully that will come later) but it is important to note here:

Discipline isn't about correcting past bad behavior as much as it should be about creating future good behavior.

God has entrusted these children into your care, but they won't always be children. Try to take the long view and recognize that your young children are going to disobey, make messes, and talk back. Your discipline should help create teenagers, young adults, and eventually adults who don't do these things as often. They should have been taught to recognize the ramifications of their behavior and not just been punished but corrected. So, view your spouse as your partner in creating really awesome people.

Another reason communication is so important here is because this season may also include moving in different directions for clubs, sports teams, and other school and extracurricular activities. We have four kids, and they are all involved in lots of activities. They each serve at our church. At one point they were at three different schools. In one season we had a baseball player, a lacrosse player, a football player, and a cheerleader. Each came with their own practice and game schedules at different fields and parks.

This can create some really fun experiences and you should enjoy it. We adjusted our dinner schedules and often ate before everyone headed in different directions. Often mom had one or two in her car and dad had the others in his car. We see those moments as opportunities to get to know our kids individually. We learned how to prompt conversation with open ended questions that spurred them to talk. Instead of asking generally, "How was your day?" we would ask, "What was your favorite thing that happened today, and what was your least favorite thing that happened today?" This gave them a chance to give a specific example, but it also gave them a chance to learn how to articulate negative experiences. When we got back home, we filled in our spouse so we were both learning the same things about our kids.

This was specific to us, and your context may bring different challenges. The key is good communication…again. It also forces you to be intentional about time for just the two of you. We talked more about this in the chapter on Fri-Dates, but you've got to find what works for you. In this season you can't allow your entire marriage to revolve exclusively around your kids. Otherwise, in future seasons when the kids aren't around, your spouse might not want to be either.

Teen Season

Don't believe the rumors. Having teenagers can be really fun. Oh, it can be infuriating, too, but it can be a lot of fun. We were youth pastors for 10 years, so we got to watch other families navigate this season, but once we got here, we still felt ill-prepared. Everyone just figures it out.

While previous seasons force you to get in sync about discipline, the teen season puts pressure on your partnership to see if you actually agree or not. We've literally had arguments about issues that had little to do with either of us. It was about something one of the kids was doing, or did, and how one of us wanted to respond to it. On more than one occasion we've had to say, "Wait a minute. This is what they want. They're trying to trick us. They want to divide us so they can get their way." We outfox the fox. That's a very good feeling.

What we have found to be a necessary priority in this season is healthy communication. Are you hearing that repeated enough yet? Our kids are all active in a variety of things. From school programs to homework to practices to games to church activities to friends, it can sometimes feel like we are cohabitating Uber drivers for the next generation. Ships passing in the night. Don't allow yourselves to get so busy that you lose one another.

In our house the biggest surprise of this season was its effect on our sex life. There are literally people up all the time. Our bedroom is on the same floor as all the kids' bedrooms. We have a few early birds and a few night owls. The early birds definitely take after Jeremy, and the night owls are usually up with Corrie. There is a short window of time in any 24-hour period where there aren't kids up and potentially walking into our room. So, you have to get creative. We talked about this in the chapter on intimacy, but a midday meet up or quiche in the bathroom, among other things, become viable options.

It sounds cliché, but this season goes by really fast. We know they all do, but this one seems to have a speed we were unprepared for. One minute you're trying to figure out how to fit another elementary school macaroni art project on the fridge and the next you're pacing near the door counting down the seconds to curfew as you watch them whip the car in the driveway and sprint up the steps. You lay awake worried about the decisions they are making as you replay some of the decisions you made not that long ago at their age.

Don't forget that your teenagers are watching you. They've been watching you their whole lives, but in this season, they are starting to have crushes and date and consider the kind of person they may want to marry one day. So much of their evaluations will be filtered through what they see in you and your marriage. There are things they will be desperate to have because your marriage embodied it. There will also be things they avoid because they saw the problems it created in your home.

Don't fake it. Authentically model something worth emulating.

Empty Nest

We have decided to include every other season under this one heading. If your kids are grown, you might be living in a season that doesn't feel like it fits under such a broad heading. However, we feel like these seasons have enough in common to put them all together.

To begin, let us restate that as of the writing of this book all of our kids still live at home, so we aren't in this season yet. However, we've done enough life with, met with, interacted with, and counseled enough couples who are in this season that we feel we can speak to it.

In this season you are figuring out how to reorient your life around something other than your kids at home. Maybe the grandkids have a ballgame, or your college or adult children are coming home to visit, but it's different than it was.

The Netflix show *The Crown* is a historical fictional account based on the life of Queen Elizabeth. The first several seasons portray her early reign, including her relationship with Prince Philip before and during the early days of their marriage. They had a lot of ups and downs, and the health of their relationship wasn't always visible to the public eye. However, the writers seem to convey that they were very much in love and had a depth to their marriage that others could not fathom.

In one episode they were at a dinner celebrating their 10th wedding anniversary and Prince Philip stands to make a speech. He says (our paraphrase), "There comes a point in marriage when you actually know the other person better than they know themselves. You see their blind spots, the good, the bad, and the ugly things that they cannot see. You have a larger view of who they are than they do."

What a powerful picture of the permission we give to our spouse in marriage. I want you to see what others see of me. I want you to see the parts of me I broadcast to the world but take special care to guard the parts of me that no one else sees, maybe not even me.

This is a high honor our spouses are giving to us. We shouldn't use their blind spots against them. We shouldn't expose their vulnerabilities or take advantage of them. To the contrary, we should do everything in our power to protect them.

In this season, start cashing the checks you've been writing all these years. That's not necessarily a financial statement. Travel, visit your family, pick up a new hobby together, and make new memories. I love hearing couples in this stage tell me they are as busy as they've ever been. Obviously, they have every right to slow down, and that may be your desired pace, but there's something really special about couples who hit this season with a healthy marriage and a larger focus on what's in front of them than what is behind them.

According to a number of studies, the years with the highest rate of divorce are year one, year seven, and year 26. That might seem like a random set of numbers, but each of those years is generally at the start of a new season. Year one would obviously be tied to the newlywed season. Year seven is most likely in the season of babies or school-age kids. Year 26 is somewhere around the start of the empty nest season.

If you think about what each of these specific seasons presents to couples, you start to see patterns that show why divorce would be more prevalent here. It's so easy to get married. You can have a big wedding that costs lots of money, but you can also stand before a justice of the peace or a cruise ship captain to say, "I do." There isn't a set of criteria required. During or just after year one, maybe you decide this isn't what you signed up for. Divorce in year seven has often been called the seven-year itch. You've been married for a while but maybe you start to think you're missing out. Perhaps there were problems and you tried to mask them by having kids. It helped for a while, but now it's multiplied what was broken in the first place. Eventually, one or both decides they can't do this anymore.

Maybe year 26 is when the kids have moved on and you look around the house and only see someone you used to know really well but aren't sure you like anymore.

We don't offer these stats as a forgone conclusion that divorce will happen, or that it will happen in those years or seasons. Instead, we offer them as a warning. You should make sure you 100 percent want to get married to this person for all the right reasons before you ever get into year one. You should build a foundation of love, respect, intimacy, and communication in the early stages of marriage that makes you excited about the years to come instead of looking for a way out. You should prioritize one another in every early season—create shared experiences, tell funny stories, and make plans for the future, so that when the nest gets empty, your tank is full.

Closing Thoughts

I (Jeremy) am not a farmer. Corrie has the green thumb and fills our home and yard with beautiful things. I can't figure out how to grow anything. But I do know—from observation, watching others, and reading the Bible—you don't sow and reap in the same season. Some seasons are obviously reaping seasons, but others are hard work. You're tilling the ground, planting seeds for later, and staring at a ground that isn't yet bearing fruit. That's the way it's supposed to be.

So often when we sit with young couples for premarital counseling, they talk about their plans to immediately have what their parents have. I love that because it usually indicates they've had great examples in marriage. However, we also caution them that their parents didn't have those things in year one. You may not be able to buy a house right away. Your honeymoon may be the only international trip you take for a few years. You may not get to set your own schedule until you're two or three more rungs up the org chart. The health of their relationship was years in the making. So be ready to do the hard work and start making your own.

Galatians 6:9 "Let us not become weary in doing good, for at the proper time we will reap a harvest if we do not give up."

In the proper time you will reap. In another season perhaps the harvest will appear. It doesn't make this season meaningless; it makes it incredibly meaningful. You WILL NOT reap in the next season, what you DO NOT sow in this season. Don't give up. Don't grow weary. The best is yet to come!

Conclusion

Don't forget your "Why"

I (Jeremy) was walking down the sidewalk at youth camp when I was 13 years old. Approaching me was a group of teenage girls about my age. Little did I know that Corrie was in that group. I just knew they were really cute, so when they passed, I turned around and started following them. I don't remember my opening line, but I'm sure it was awesome. One conversation led to another conversation, which led to late nights talking and then to AOL Instant Messenger. Eventually, our emails led to text messages and phone calls which became dinners and dates which led us to "I do." We didn't know at 13 we would get married, and perhaps you didn't know right away at 18 or 25 or 35 you would get married. And yet, there was a length of time and a process where we fell in love and decided we'd found the person we wanted to spend the rest of our lives with.

Ephesians 5:31-32 As the Scriptures say, "A man leaves his father and mother and is joined to his wife, and the two are united into one." This is a great mystery, but it is an illustration of the way Christ and the church are one.

We opened this book talking about love stories. Often our lives don't feel like these grand stories. They feel like Tuesday trips to the grocery store and Saturday yard work and raising kids and saving for college and so much more. But what if we told you your marriage is telling God's love story to the whole world? Not a Hallmark movie. Not the latest Netflix series.

Christ and the Church.

The reason we believe so much in healthy marriages is because you have the potential to point people to Jesus by the way you love each other. Reframing our marriages in this way changes everything.

John 13:34-35 "A new command I give you: Love one another. As I have loved you, so you must love one another. By this everyone will know that you are my disciples, if you love one another."

What if we reframed marriage this way?

"As I have loved you, so you must love _____ *(insert the name of your spouse).***"**

I (Jeremy) watched this play out in my childhood home on a regular basis. As I have mentioned several times I grew up in a home with a great marriage. In watching my mom love my dad, my dad love my mom, and my parents love me and Jason, I literally learned about the love of Jesus. I have never really struggled to believe that Jesus loves me because of the context in which I was raised. I recognize not everyone had that reality. Our home was filled with a love for one another that started with my parents and translated to Jesus.

If we, the Church, are described as the bride of Christ in scripture, then we can believe that our job is to embody Godly love towards the world, starting with our spouse. If I view Corrie as a recipient of God's love through the way I love her, it puts the challenge on me to receive God's love personally and give God's love freely. It helps me to think that my kids will know more about God's love by the way they see me loving their mom. Husbands, that's a challenge worth accepting!

I (Corrie) mentioned earlier that I grew up in a home with a single mom and two sisters. While mom has apologized at different times for some of the decisions she made, I think she did an amazing job. She raised three strong women. She had a good career and with the help of the Lord was able to provide for our every need. I'm incredibly thankful for my mom. Other than Jeremy, she's my best friend.

Without a doubt the best thing she did for us was keep us in church. In fact, she didn't just keep us in church, she kept us in the same church my whole life. For the most part, the same people who knew me as a baby taught me in Sunday school and prayed for me in the youth group. That stability proved invaluable to my development.

My church is where I learned how to read the Bible. I learned how to pray there. I made lifelong friends there. However, perhaps the greatest impact on my life was being able to watch the married couples there. Because I didn't have a Godly example of marriage in my home, I had to look elsewhere. It wasn't a formal thing, and I didn't walk up to married couples to ask, "Can I watch how healthy your marriage is so I'll know what I should do one day?" I just watched Sunday after Sunday, month after month, and year after year. I watched my pastor and his wife. I watched the parents of my friends. I watched older couples who sat near me in church. I watched how they spoke to each other, and I watched them pray for one another.

They didn't even know I was watching, but I would think to myself or pray to the Lord, "That's what I want." They modeled for me what it looked like to love one another in the way God intended.

A few years ago, Jeremy and I were walking around the mall with some of my family. We were in a clothing store and, as Jeremy and I were laughing about something, he leaned over and kissed my forehead. I didn't even know she was watching but I found out later that my niece leaned over to my mom, pointed to us, and said, "That's what I want." I don't say that with any pride whatsoever. We aren't perfect, but it was a full circle moment. That young girl saw something in another couple that she wants for her future. I am humbled to think our relationship has impacted someone else the way someone else's marriage impacted me.

God could have used any mechanism, apparatus, or relationship to show His love, but He chose marriage to point people to His Son. That reality should force us to reconsider how we treat our spouse. It should change what we argue about. It should change what we prioritize.

Your marriage *is* telling a great love story.

Who is watching you? If you have children, whether they live in your house or not, they're watching. There are probably little girls and boys at your church watching your love story play out. Some of them have great examples in their own homes, but others don't. There are people on your street watching your marriage. They see you run the trashcans down to the road late at night in your pajamas. They hear your conversation as you take your evening walks on the sidewalk in front of their house. They're listening as you call your kids in for dinner. What is your love story telling them?

Who is saying, "That's what I want," as they watch you?

Perhaps you've gotten all the way to this point in the book and your marriage isn't telling this kind of love story. It's not too late! In fact, we are incredibly thankful for you. We've prayed for you. It's not by accident you're reading this. God desires to capture your heart, and your spouse's heart, and draw you each closer to Him than you've ever been before. The amazing benefit of this reality is that you will draw closer to one another in the process.

It doesn't matter if you're engaged, newly married, have young kids at home, argue with teenagers about curfew, or live in an empty nest—your marriage matters. It matters to God. It matters to us. It should matter to you. It's not too late to make it matter. Start living a marriage that inspires others. Start living a marriage that points people to Jesus. And start living a marriage that tells a better story…

Right now!

YOUR NOTES

_____

_____

_____

_____

_____

_____

_____

_____

_____

_____

_____

_____

_____

_____

_____

_____

_____

Made in the USA
Columbia, SC
09 September 2022

66754925R00102